THE DEATH OF SLAVERY

The Death

THE CHICAGO HISTORY OF AMERICAN CIVILIZATION

Daniel J. Boorstin, EDITOR

# of Slavery

The United States, 1837–65

By Elbert B. Smith

 THE UNIVERSITY OF CHICAGO PRESS

CHICAGO AND LONDON

Library of Congress Catalog Card Number: 67–16779

THE UNIVERSITY OF CHICAGO PRESS, CHICAGO & LONDON
The University of Toronto Press, Toronto 5, Canada

to

Jean
with love

Editor's Preface

The coming of the Civil War has been distorted by two kinds of hindsight. First, there has been the argument that the war was "inevitable." Nothing is more difficult than imagining that things could have been otherwise. Second, there has been the argument that the war was a simple conflict between Good and Evil. The Americans fighting for the Union, we are told, were consciously engaged in a holy crusade, while those on the other side were conscious champions of slavery. To ask ourselves simply, "Why was the war inevitable?" or "Why were so many Americans against freedom?" is to miss the actual experience of most of the people of those years. To sense what it was really like to be alive then, we must try to see the choices those men saw.

Elbert B. Smith, in this history of the United States from 1837 to 1865, puts his spotlight on the actual choices that men faced. He is more interested in what they saw ahead of them

Editor's Preface

than in what we can see behind us. Mr. Smith has the great advantage over most historians of the era, that he has personally immersed himself in the democratic process. Having run for elective office, he has seen what kinds of issues do, and do not, reach the people. By his grasp of the intriguing intricacies of political history, he helps us understand how personal strengths and weaknesses made certain issues seem crucial, and certain compromises impossible. The Civil War, according to Mr. Smith, cannot be adequately summarized as the product either of inevitability or of morality.

In the later twentieth century we should not need to be reminded that the Civil War left many questions unsettled. The travail of our own time—our continuing struggle to realize the ideals of our Founders—should remind us that to oversimplify any era in history is to befog the tasks of later generations.

The "Chicago History of American Civilization" aims to bring to the general reader, in compact and readable form, the insights of scholars who write from different points of view. This series contains two kinds of books: a *chronological* group, which will provide a coherent narrative of American history from its beginning to the present day, and a *topical* group which will deal with the history of varied and significant aspects of American life. This is a volume in the chronological group. Those which have already been published are listed at the end of this volume.

DANIEL J. BOORSTIN

Table of Contents

I

Historians Have Said...

During the period 1837–65, the United States endured depressions, enjoyed immense progress and prosperity, and acquired a vast western empire in a foreign war. The democratic ideology enunciated by Jefferson and brought to a climax by the time of Andrew Jackson continued to gain strength and become a vital part of the American scene. Political parties won and lost elections, national policies often succeeded and sometimes failed, many conflicts were settled by debate and compromise, and many remained unsettled. Meanwhile, the population grew and prospered on its patrimony of magnificent natural resources and almost unlimited space.

In 1861, however, this idyllic scene was shattered by the guns of Fort Sumter, and more than 600,000 men died before peace was restored. This overshadowing event by necessity becomes the central theme of any history of this period.

The Death of Slavery

Any study dealing with the coming of the American Civil War is certain to provide more unanswerable questions than unquestionable answers. Why did the democratic system of debate, compromise, and acceptance of compromise—a system whereby Americans were supposed to settle their quarrels, competitions, and conflicts with words instead of weapons— break down in 1861? Why did men who shared a common heritage, common language, and common loyalties finally resort to that most undemocratic of all expedients, war? Was the war inevitable? Was it necessary? Do those who argue that perhaps the war was unnecessary deserve the usual accusation that they are insufficiently alert to the moral evil of slavery? Could the wicked institution of slavery have been destroyed without the carnage of war? Did the differences in geography, climate, economic development, and social institutions make necessary the deaths of more than 600,000 Americans and the suffering of millions of others?

Is the study of this period in American life a mere survey of great sweeping impersonal deterministic forces which shaped human destinies regardless of what men as individuals could have done? Certainly the long growing season and warmer weather affected the development of the South. The cold winters, rocky soil, rugged coastline, and rich industrial power from swiftly flowing rivers shaped the character of New England. The economic versatility and the cosmopolitan character of the population of the middle Atlantic states and certain border states made them strongholds of the spirit of compromise. The wealth of resources to the west, coupled with magnificent natural systems of water transportation, helped make an interdependent nation and create a northwestern region ready to fight for the preservation of a national union. The very existence of slavery in an exuberant new land dedicated to freedom and equality of opportunity, and racing toward the technological miracles of the twentieth century, was an anachronism which could have no future. And hovering over all was a religious tradition which divided the world into good and evil and forbade compromise on questions involving moral righteousness and wickedness.

Modern man, however, is compelled to seek a faith in the existence of a wide variety and range of independent human behavior within the limits of such determinisms. The belief that man is a free moral agent who will succeed or fail, prosper or suffer, and survive or be destroyed on the basis of his own actions, is necessary for responsible human behavior at any level. This belief is also man's best antidote to intolerant ideologies whose followers claim to be in step with the world's predetermined future and thereby derive special authority to inflict cruelties against their fellowmen. The deterministic view of history all too often produces either the pessimist who sees no value in constructive effort or the fanatic eager to shape the world to his own pattern regardless of the cost.

If, therefore, the years leading to America's great tragedy are to shed useful light on the dilemmas of the modern world, the situations, decisions, actions, and events of the period must be viewed as manmade or at least man-affected phenomena which might have been different and which need not be repeated. Some historians have called this period the first cold war. Those who would help keep the present cold war from ending like the first can learn much from a careful study of this earlier American experience.

Immediately following the American Civil War, each section, naturally enough, wrote its own story of why it all happened. In the North the war became a great crusade fought to free

The Death of Slavery

human beings from bondage. In the history texts Northern heroes led by the martyr Abraham Lincoln joined a noble struggle against the immoral, undemocratic, and unchristian evil of slavery and marched away to die to make men free. The war ended slavery; the war, therefore, was fought for that purpose.

This soul-satisfying, heart-warming, inspiring, but grossly oversimplified view still has its warm defenders. In the modern version, the South never would have abandoned slavery without war; slavery was a moral evil too wicked for toleration by civilized men; those, therefore, who question the inevitability of the war and suggest the possibility of an eventually peaceful settlement are sentimental appeasers unwilling to come to grips with harsh realities.

This interpretation, however, is badly weakened by the admitted fact that most Northern leaders in 1861, including Lincoln, emphatically denied any inclination to injure Southern slavery. The Republican presidential convention of 1860 passed over the party's longtime leader, William H. Seward, because of his connections with radical abolitionism, and the party's platform contained pledges that Southern slavery would remain undisturbed. Lincoln's speeches, including his first inaugural address, repeated this theme over and over. Indeed, Lincoln also pledged himself as President to enforce the federal laws designed to help Southerners recover fugitive slaves. When General Frémont, in the early part of the war, freed the slaves in Missouri by proclamation, Lincoln promptly revoked the action and discharged Frémont lest Missouri be driven to secession. "My paramount object in this struggle," Lincoln wrote Horace Greeley in 1862, "is to save the Union and *is not* either to save or destroy slavery. If I could save the Union without freeing

4

any slaves, I would do it; if I could save it by freeing *all* the slaves, I would do it; and if I could do it by freeing some and leaving others alone, I would also do that."

Abraham Lincoln spoke for a northwestern region which practiced various proscriptions against free Negroes and which objected to slavery primarily for economic reasons. He also spoke for men everywhere who were dedicated to the preservation of the national state created by the founding fathers. Such men were driven by the powerful spirit of nationalism which swept through the nineteenth century world to create national states in Germany and Italy and leave a powerful desire for national independence among subject peoples everywhere.

Nationalism had a further dimension in the United States. To Lincoln and many other Americans the United States was a great experiment in freedom and self-government which for the sake of the entire human race must not be allowed to fail. Those honored at Gettysburg, said Lincoln in his immortal address, had died that "government of the people, by the people, for the people, shall not perish from the earth."

Southern secession threatened to destroy this experiment by proving the incompatibility of democracy and national unity, and slavery thereby became a symbol of disunion which must be destroyed for the salvation of America itself. Then and then only did abolition become a practical threat to Southern slavery.

Southern radicals, however, refused to believe Lincoln's assurances. They made the right to expand slavery into new territories a test of future Northern intentions, and when Lincoln and his party refused to yield on this question they struck for an independent South.

That the fire-eaters reached such a decision is less remarkable than their ability to get the Southern people to follow it, since only a fourth of them had any direct relation with slavery. In the end the Southern excuse for secession was a denial of the right to take slavery into territories where the institution would have been virtually impossible because of geography, climate, or the attitudes of the people already there.

The most popular Southern version has rested largely upon the constitutional defense of Alexander H. Stephens and Jefferson Davis. According to this view the Constitution guaranteed slavery, the North refused to abide by these constitutional principles, and the South, therefore, was compelled to leave the Union for its own protection. John C. Calhoun and the Southern extremists, runs this interpretation, were really great nationalists who strove to preserve the Union of the founding fathers and left it only when the North had converted it into an instrument of tyranny against the Southern way of life.

This interpretation, like the popular Northern view, is much too simple. To be sure, the Constitution recognized slavery by awarding the South white representatives in Congress for three-fifths of the slave population. It protected slavery as property under the due process of law clause, and no one seriously questioned the constitutionality of federal laws designed to help recapture fugitive slaves. The timeless idealism of the Declaration of Independence, which says that *all* men are created free and equal, was not copied into the infinitely more conservative Constitution. The freedom-granting Thirteenth, Fourteenth, and Fifteenth Amendments did not come until after the Civil War. The abolitionist, William Lloyd Garrison, once burned the Constitution publicly and pronounced it "a covenant with death and an agreement with hell." William H. Seward became famous for his talk about the "higher law" of God which placed human freedom above all legal documents and manmade laws, and therefore outranked the Constitution on the subject of slavery.

When Southerners, however, sought to extend their constitutional doctrines to the question of taking slavery to new territories, they were on weak ground. Indeed, the South finally worked itself into a constitutional dilemma. Its leaders presented a states' rights argument for a federal government too weak to keep slavery out of new territories, and in the next breath demanded a federal government with power to impose slavery on new territories regardless of the wishes of the inhabitants. In the 1840's, John C. Calhoun spun his involved doctrines against the right of the federal government to prohibit territorial slavery. Yet the Northwest Ordinance of 1787, which barred slavery in the area north of the Ohio River, and the Missouri Compromise of 1820, which barred slavery in the vast area north of the southern border of Missouri between the Mississippi River and the Rockies, had been written and overwhelmingly supported by Southerners. Likewise, in the Compromise debates of 1850 the South openly accepted the right of the federal government to prohibit slavery in the territories. In 1857 the "new" Southern position was upheld by the Supreme Court in the Dred Scott case, but the many decades of Southern acceptance and support of the earlier principle invalidated it as a justification for war.

The Southern social system and way of life were indeed being threatened, but not by Northern abolitionists. Americans were on their way to a new world of scientific and technological miracles—an industrial world with which an agrarian way of life built upon slavery could not compete and an ideological world in which human slavery would be intolerable.

The Death of Slavery

Threats and fears are more endurable, however, when they can be identified in terms of enemies who can be seen, understood, and fought against directly. Northern opponents of slavery provided Southerners with simple, emotionally satisfying, but dangerous answers to the difficult problems that would eventually have to be faced. The suffering and destruction of the Civil War would neither solve the problems nor make them easier.

As time passed, historians who continued to see the war as a crusade against slavery found forgiveness for the South in the forces of climate, geography, and soils which had enabled the institution to thrive. In this view slavery was a burden rather than a sin, and the Southerners were victims of circumstances. James Ford Rhodes blamed the technology of cotton-raising. Woodrow Wilson found the war to be a product of growth and evolution. Southerners like William E. Dodd and Ulrich B. Phillips defended their section as one of many virtues which had done its best with its faults and problems. Other Southerners like Frank Owsley and Charles Ramsdell continued to reject the olive branch.

The deterministic philosophy so prevalent at the turn of the nineteenth century ultimately produced the view of Charles Beard and various followers that slavery did not cause the war at all. These writers saw the Civil War as the final stage in the ancient quarrel between Hamilton and Jefferson over whether America would become a land of commerce and industry or remain dominated by agriculture. In this view the North wanted a powerful, unified, paternalistic central government which could provide high tariffs, sound national banking, the removal of immigration barriers and easy importation of foreign labor, subsidies to railroad builders, uniform protection for business in all the states, and sundry other services. Because the agrarian South had successfully opposed all these things in the name of states' rights but had begun to feel its power slipping, and because the North was determined to have these policies, the two sections eventually went to war to settle the question. This interpretation is important. Certainly economic competition contributed much to the animosities which brought on the war. This version, however, reads result into causation and as a single explanation is grossly inadequate. It exaggerates the economic uniformity within each section, ignores the Northwest as a separate section, and incorrectly minimizes the great moral question of slavery and the emotional drive of nationalism. Indeed, the United States in the 1850's had already demonstrated a remarkable capacity for producing industrial wealth without significant government assistance.

Economic differences were compromised when moral issues were not involved, but the question of extending slavery created a point beyond which compromises could not go. Sacrificing personal integrity by compromising moral right and wrong is difficult for honest men anywhere, and nineteenth-century Americans were thoroughly steeped in the tradition of religious salvation through righteousness and eternal damnation through wickedness. To argue that Americans might have had a civil war without the slavery quarrel is nonsense. Moreover, the men who flocked to the colors to put down Southern armed rebellion and save the Union did not see themselves as part of an economic contest, and neither did Abraham Lincoln.

A related interpretation has blamed the war on deep-seated social, economic, and psychological differences. Certainly the industrial Northeast differed from the agrarian South, and the

9

The Death of Slavery

Northwest differed from both, but Americans in 1861 were far more alike than different. A majority in every state, including those of the South, were small, independent farmers. Americans spoke the same language, joined the same nationwide church organizations, voted for and against the same political parties, loved the same flag, sang the same "Star-Spangled Banner," and loved the same Union. They shared a common history, economic interdependence, and kinfolk in every section. Cultural differences alone in a nation already noted for its melting pot characteristics would not have produced a civil war.

The horrors of World War I and its disillusioning aftermath, the threats to democracy inherent in the fanaticisms of Fascism and Communism, the world's journey to the brink of destruction in World War II, and the continuing threat of the cold war, created an atmosphere for the development of a new approach to the Civil War. Beginning in the late 1930's, historians like Avery Craven, James Randall, and Allan Nevins began questioning the inevitability of the war and stressing the mistakes, failures, and hypocrisies of the political leaders and opinion-makers in both sections. In this "revisionist" view the war became a breakdown in the democratic system of government brought about in part by growing economic, social, and value differences, and in part by the creation of false images of each section in the eyes of the other; events and situations were distorted and exaggerated by partisan politicians, the press, writers, and the churches, until ordinary people and generations of later historians completely lost sight of the actual facts.

The revisionist historians exploded many earlier myths and produced historical narratives infinitely more accurate in detail. They also made a powerful case for moderation, gradual and non-violent progress, avoidance of fanaticism, responsibility in partisan politics, and the long view of history.

Their chances for a universal following, however, foundered on the insoluble question of slavery. Various Southern critics remained unwilling to admit that men had died to defend an institution not necessarily in danger. Northerners were reluctant to surrender their glow of moral superiority to a view which reduced the sentiments of the "Battle Hymn of the Republic" to an afterthought. The revisionists were charged with blindness to the moral evil of slavery and were compelled by the logic of their position to argue that slavery might have been tolerated for a few more years and that the institution might have died peacefully if the war had been avoided. Abraham Lincoln had once taken exactly the same position. The first argument, however, was subject to easy distortion, and the second was unprovable. Among the critics, Kenneth Stampp and others dwelt on the profitability of slavery and argued that it might have gone on forever without the war, while Arthur Schlesinger, Jr., drew upon the world's sad experience with appeasement of the Nazis during the 1930's to conclude that in 1861 violence was the only realistic solution to an inescapable moral dilemma.

Few, however, could quarrel with the basic revisionist theme that men should strive for peaceful solutions even to their most difficult problems and irreconcilable conflicts and that such solutions become more difficult when truth, realism, and rational calculations of interest succumb to emotionalism, pride, and fears based upon partisan distortions and exaggerations. Even fewer could fail to hope that these lessons of the nineteenth century would not be wasted upon the twentieth.

11

II

There Were Sections

The New England corner of the United States is a region of granite and ice. In past ages the glaciers covered the land with rocks and a thin topsoil which would offer little to future farmers. Certain compensating resources remained, however. Swift rivers would turn factory wheels and later produce electricity. A rugged coastline with deep bays and many islands provided great harbors for oceangoing trade. Magnificent forests of conifers and hardwoods provided the timbers for the greatest sailing vessels ever built by man. Great underwater banks furnished a rich harvest of fish. Colonial New Englanders soon developed into woodworkers, furniture-makers, shipbuilders, sailors, fishermen, and tradesmen.

For the early settlers New England was a rough, stingy, cold environment, but the English Calvinist Puritans were more than a match for it. They had left sinful England to prove that in a new world men could build a holy commonwealth ruled by the laws of God. They considered their problems and misfortunes to be God's testing devices, and hard work and endurance of adversity provided opportunities for proving their election to the kingdom of heaven. The holy commonwealth required constant attention to the ills and evils of society, as well as to the morals of its citizens, and it was no coincidence that most of the great mid-nineteenth-century reform movements in America originated in New England. New Englanders stressed self-examination, schools, churches, and social responsibility. Calvinist theology taught that man was naturally depraved, and that though creating wealth was godly, enjoying it was sinful. Wealth, after all, was a gift from God, and its possessor was to administer it as a steward administers the property of his employer. Indeed, almost any pleasure, because of its temptations to excess, was dangerous. Even the doctrine that unbaptized infants were condemned to hellfire was still preached in the early nineteenth century. The New England God was a god of anger, unbending justice, and adequate punishment, who divided men into the righteous and unrighteous and had little time for the in-between.

The industrial boom triggered by the War of 1812 brought new ways of living to New England. The earlier small factories gave way to major industries, and the region soon found itself with the problems as well as the advantages of urban industrialism.

The first labor supply came from the farms. New England industrialization coincided with a great population thrust into western New York and the Great Lakes region, and this opening of new soils gave New England agriculture severe competition. Many rural young people either joined the trek westward or moved into the industrial towns and cities.

Soon long black wagons, the original Black Marias, were going up and down the villages picking up young girls for work in the new textile mills. Recruiting advertisements promised parents their daughters would live in closely supervised dormitories, be marched regularly to church, and be carefully regulated as to moral habits. The image of factory work as a highly moral and religious experience aided substantially in the recruitment of thousands of new laborers, poetically described by Whittier as the "fair, unveiled nuns of industry."

Young men also worked in the factories, as well as a great many wives and children. Factories would hire entire families by contracting with the father for the services of his household. In 1820, 45 per cent of the workers in New England factories were children under twelve. Wages and working conditions varied from place to place, and in some areas there was genuine enlightenment, but generally the hours were long and the pay was low.

In the beginning, however, there was considerable harmony among employers and employees. The young laborers were often fugitives from cold, harsh, and lonely farms, and the opportunity to work twelve to fourteen hours a day in the company of other young people seemed an improvement over their previous life. Also, the early industrial leaders were often men who knew their workers personally and were endowed with a considerable sense of social responsibility.

Time, however, soon produced a new generation of workers who had no memories of an older way of life and who wanted more and better things for themselves. Simultaneously, British competition was driving down the price of cotton cloth all over the world, and employers were finding themselves less rather than more willing to grant either higher wages or better working conditions. Also, the factory builders and their heirs were in many cases moving from the factory towns to the more luxurious coastal cities like Boston and Newport and were leaving their industries in the hands of managers responsible only for profits. All this helped bring to New England many of the worst features of industrialism in its early stages: periodic depressions and unemployment, relatively low wages and poor working conditions, poverty, insecurity for the sick and the aged, slums, juvenile delinquency, crime, and labor conflicts.

Employers frequently found it easier to change workers than to change conditions. Wagons began to bring in French Canadian girls to spin the cloth, and ships began to unload young Irish men and women by the hundreds. The fierce competition for jobs was compounded by the fact that most of the newcomers were Roman Catholics, and ancient religious conflicts were soon revived in all their bitterness.

The New England transition to a new way of life was painful, but among people reared in the Calvinist tradition it provided the impetus for the greatest age of reform in American history. Throughout New England and indeed throughout the entire Northeast, new attitudes swept through the churches and intellectual circles. Religious leaders in great revival movements as well as in the older churches began stressing the gospel of Christ in terms of the duty of men to help and serve each other. Some like William Ellery Channing formed the new Unitarian Church, which almost entirely ignored the supernatural and put its faith in religion as a way of life on earth rather than as a ticket to heaven. Others became agnostics in the pattern of the labor reformers Robert Dale Owen and

The Death of Slavery

Frances Wright. Ralph Waldo Emerson led the transcendentalists, who believed that the essential nobility of man's nature transcended his experience and environment. Emerson felt that man was in every way created in the image of God and that there was no height unattainable by man. Indeed, most of the reformers of the period shared this new faith in the essential perfectibility of man as well as the duty of every man to work for a more perfect world.

Freedom's ferment occasionally took unusual shapes. Joseph Smith of Vermont discovered the golden books of Mormon and founded a religious sect noted for the collective economic responsibility assumed by its members. The practice of polygamy brought persecution which pushed the saints across the continent until they founded their own state of Utah. For others seeking escape there was William Miller, whose biblical scholarship led him to the conclusion that Christ would return in 1843 to gather up the faithful, raise the dead, and reward the saints. Aided somewhat by the tail of a comet which throughout 1843 hung across the noonday sky like a poised sword, Miller won more than a million converts. On the appointed day many of the Millerites gave away property, tearfully bade loved ones good-bye, donned their white ascension robes, and waited for a judgment that did not come. The effort to avoid an evil world and return to true principles led also to various communal experiments like Brook Farm, Fruitlands, New Harmony, and the Oneida community. Most of these efforts failed because of poor organization, the frequently impractical nature of the participants, and the reluctance of members to accept the standard of living imposed by independent isolation.

For most reformers, however, building God's earthly kingdom meant a concern for better schools, hospitals, and prisons;

movements against liquor, tobacco, cruelty to animals, and war; movements for women's rights and better living for working people; and, finally, opposition to the great evil of human slavery. In countless editorials, propaganda sheets, sermons, speeches, poems, and books, and through associations, societies, and political movements, the work went forward and carried itself to a climax, oddly enough, in a crusade against an institution which did not even exist in the region.

Much of central and western New York was settled by New Englanders, and the same religious and intellectual ferment spread quickly through that region. New York cities came to share the same industrial problems. New York politics were characterized also by struggles between the great harbor city and the rural areas and by struggles between the owners of the big landed estates and the smaller farmers. New York had been one of the least democratic of the American colonies, and the years of conflict spent correcting this situation left the state one of the most democratic in the Union. By the 1840's the Whig party had abandoned its earlier conservative image and was competing with the Jacksonian Democrats for the votes of workingmen as well as liberal reformers. The Whig governor and senator, William H. Seward, and his alter ego, editor Thurlow Weed, adopted first the emotionalism of anti-Masonry and then the twin spirits of abolitionism and Free-Soilism as instruments in their programs for defeating the "Albany regency" led by Martin Van Buren. As governor, senator, and President, Van Buren was a Jeffersonian agrarian who appealed to farmers with conservative hard-money economics and to workingmen with a powerful democratic ideology. The Whigs served the growing industrial interests, and advocated all the paternalistic federal programs opposed by Van Buren. As Van

The Death of Slavery

Buren's economic principles became less and less applicable to the needs and ambitions of New Yorkers, Seward and Weed found their key to success by adding a new liberal political philosophy. In the end the quest for votes drove many Van Burenites into a partnership with the Whigs in the movement against the extension of slavery.

Pennsylvania was further removed from the unique mind and conscience of New England, and had enjoyed a far more democratic colonial experience than New York. Like New York it was rich in both agricultural and industrial resources. Pennsylvania touched the Great Lakes at its northwestern tip, but it was intimately tied to the southern and middle states by the Ohio River. Andrew Jackson had made the Democratic party a powerful force in Pennsylvania, and, as in New York, the Whigs moved away from political conservatism while working for their traditional aims of high tariff, federal internal improvements, and a United States Bank. Western Pennsylvania was the great hive from which thousands of frontier families had swarmed up and down the valleys, into the South as well as the Northwest. Its people had many ties of kinship in both sections.

Essentially a border state and looking in both directions economically, Pennsylvania was also a state in which the spirit of nationalism burned bright and clear. In general, Pennsylvanians took a tolerant attitude toward their slaveholding brethren, and it was perhaps no coincidence that Pennsylvania's most important antebellum spokesman and leader was James Buchanan, the peace-seeking compromiser often denounced as a Northern President with Southern principles.

New Jersey shared in the new economic developments of New York and eastern Pennsylvania. The Presbyterian college at Princeton and the Dutch Reformed college called Rutgers

18

helped foster the spirit of John Calvin, but both were less dominated by reforming spirit than Harvard and other New England counterparts. The political parties in New Jersey were fairly evenly matched, but Whig economics were in the ascendancy.

The Northeast, then, was a varied section characterized by eager acceptance of new technology and by rapid industrialization. Even before the American Revolution it had abandoned slavery, but urbanism and industrialization were creating new problems of their own. These in turn were creating in various parts of the region a great age of isms and reforms. The region was caught in something of an inner conflict between the appeal of Democratic political ideology and the desire for Whig economic policies, but the Whig party was doing much to ease this tension by becoming more democratic.

The region had a connection with slavery through the shiploads of Southern cotton which provided raw materials for the textile mills and factories, but slavery and slaveholders were not economic competitors either real or potential. For the Northeast slavery was a distant but all-absorbing evil to be added to the list of dragons against which a generation of reformers had already drawn their swords. The economic and ideological characteristics of the Northeast were destined to set the pattern of the future in American life, and the compulsion to oppose slavery and its extension was certain to spread and gain strength as a result.

The antebellum South was a land of great variety in soils, climate, topography, and economic and social life. Certain general characteristics and problems, however, tended to give it unity. The weather was warm and hence the growing season

19

lasted longer. The rainfall was heavier and more frequent. The soils were in the beginning reasonably fertile, but they were subject to heavy depletion from erosion and excessive one-crop production. The agrarian economic base which supported all the early American colonies lasted long and resisted change in the South because of its success and because of a labor system which became also a social institution. The original shipload of frightened African captives had been increased by 1860 to some 4,215,000 slaves in a total population of 11,133,361.

Slavery solved two problems for white Southerners. It was a very important labor system for those engaged in agriculture on any significant scale. It was particularly useful in developing the Southern frontier into a vast cotton kingdom, where the slave's capacity for heavy work in intense heat was put to the maximum use.

The system, however, was expensive and often wasteful. Slaves cost a great deal of money, and they and their families required subsistence from the cradle to the grave. Large-scale agriculture provided many opportunities for looking busy while doing little, and slavery provided little incentive for conscientious work.

Historians will quarrel forever over the profitability of slavery. The sum total of their efforts to date has been reasonable proof that some people in some parts of the South at certain periods found slavery immensely profitable, whereas for others it was a very heavy economic burden. In 1830 Senator Thomas Hart Benton, who owned or had owned slaves in North Carolina, Tennessee, Virginia, and Missouri, was certain slavery would eventually disappear for economic reasons, and twenty-six years later he had not changed his mind. Benton viewed the difference in race as the only force keeping the institution and the sectional conflict alive.

There Were Sections

The question of profit, however, was purely academic from the viewpoint of most Southerners. Only one Southerner in four owned slaves or had any direct contact with slavery at all. The vast number of non-slaveholding Southerners who supported and thereby made possible the secession and war in 1861 were not offering their lives in defense of slavery because of its profitability.

For slaveholder and non-slaveholder alike, the institution solved the problem of controlling some four million persons of a different color who, through no fault of their own, had been kept for two centuries in a state of captivity, forced labor, and cultural inferiority. In one sense, the slave suffered to an infinitely greater degree the same animosities visited upon the Northern immigrant laborer, but the white immigrant had the immeasurable advantage of being able to disappear through social absorption once he had improved his economic status. The slave had neither education nor property and was denied both. His resulting inferior way of life was then used as a reason for enforcing these prohibitions still further. No one could know just what social and economic convulsions would occur if he should be emancipated, and the speculations concerning such an event were compounded from fear and subconscious guilt and drew heavily upon the frightful race war which had occurred in Haiti at the turn of the century. Fear and rationality are natural enemies, and Southern fears were real enough.

Indeed, any assessment of the profitability of slavery must recognize also its deadening effect upon economic innovation or progress. In seeking to maintain a thriving atmosphere for slavery the South feared and resisted all changes which might weaken the technological and economic basis of the system. And for that matter many parts of the South have continued throughout the century since Appomattox to resist desperately needed progress which might also weaken the bonds of extra-legal inferiority pressed upon the former slave and his descendants since the Civil War. The blinding of Southern eyes and the setting of the Southern mind against the realities of the modern world ultimately cost the South more than all the profits ever made by slavery.

Brazil, where slavery was an economic institution almost divorced from racial implications, abandoned the institution without conflict. The United States, with far more liberal and humane political and social traditions, could not make the same peaceful transition. This fact merely adds to the evidence that slavery as a social rather than an economic institution was the heart of the civilization Southerners were prepared to die for in 1861. Had the slave been white, or had Americans shared the racial unconcern of their Brazilian neighbors, there would have been no American Civil War.

In response to Northern attacks the South ultimately turned to Genesis and to amateur anthropology in defense of slavery. The factor which probably did most to ease Southern consciences, however, was the basic economic security provided for most slaves. Reasonable kindness, however condescending, came naturally to most Southerners, as it did to most Americans everywhere. And beyond these considerations, to mistreat or neglect a slave was to mistreat or neglect an enormous financial investment. The well-treated, well-fed, reasonably happy slave was of infinitely greater value than one requiring constant supervision, policing, or medical care. The usual slave diet was monotonous, but it was more adequate than that of most laboring people in the mid-nineteenth century world. In most cases, also, it was shared by the young and old as well as the productive. Slave housing was crude and often dirty, but usually dry. Masters and slaves alike endured the same atrocious medical treatment, but they shared equally in the best available. Southerners never tired of comparing the security and stability of slave life to the frequent poverty, unemployment, and general misery of many free laborers in the American Northeast as well as abroad. Also, the extremely limited opportunities available to free Negroes in many Northern as well as Southern states enabled Southerners to make numerous comparisons between the happy existence enjoyed by slaves and the misery endured by former slaves who had gained their freedom.

This security plus adequate time and opportunity for sexual activity apparently did keep a majority of the slaves at least acquiescent, just as the same elements have often kept other large populations living placidly under the most stultifying political dictatorships.

For those members of any society who prefer the responsibilities of self-direction, however, slavery is obviously a frightful way of life. By its very security and by its severe limitations upon the achievement of his potential as a human being, slavery robbed the slave of the right to worry and to dream. Enforced illiteracy may be a minor imposition upon those uninterested in reading, but its impact upon a gifted mind can hardly be measured. Likewise, the narrow horizons that provide satisfactory vistas for some can be dungeon walls for those with initiative and curiosity. Perhaps only those who have been moved to explore continents, oceans, skies, and the great scientific mysteries can fully understand the tragedy of those forbidden to explore beyond the next hill.

The intelligent male slave on one of the relatively few large plantations might aspire to the status of a minor overseer,

The Death of Slavery

mechanic, artisan, or coachman. He might even become a personal body servant or valet. On extremely rare occasions a talented slave might even be permitted to carve statuary and other decorations for the master's house, but the names of such artists were not bequeathed to posterity. The female slave of ability might become a personal maid, chambermaid, or nursemaid, and, rarely, through personal relations with the family she might with the passing of the years assume the character of a "mammy," entrusted with unusual authority and responsibility. Even these limited positions, however, were far beyond the hopes of the average slave.

More obvious were the evils stressed by Northern critics. They were not common, but they were always possible and they did occur. Slaves could be whipped and otherwise cruelly mistreated despite protective laws and the pressures of public opinion. Husbands, wives, and children could be separated by sale. The laws of marriage were not mandatory, and licentiousness for the sole purpose of providing new slaves for the market could be encouraged. Comelier females could be subjected to the whims of masters and overseers. In a nation dedicated in theory at least to the essential value of every individual, even one of these occurrences made slavery a relic of barbarism.

And finally, if power has a corrupting influence, then surely the absolute ownership of other men was an unholy devil gnawing at the otherwise rational, humane, and civilized instincts of a great many Southerners. The strident demands of Southern leaders for slave rights in territories where no slaveholder intended to go, and the unreal Southern arguments for secession in the face of Northern assurances that slavery would not be disturbed, were part of a mentality conditioned at least in part by the very nature of slavery. The delusions of grandeur

There Were Sections

which led some Southerners to visualize a great Southern slave empire encompassing the Caribbean, Mexico, and Central America were cut from the same cloth. In addition to economic interest and genuine fears of a convulsive racial conflict, the simple fear of losing a status of power and inherent superiority over large numbers of other people was a significant part of the Southern attachment to slavery and remains part of the present pattern of discrimination. The arguments of John C. Calhoun to the contrary, slavery did not create a higher breed of humanity among the master race.

The generation of Southerners who fought and died because of slavery, however, did not create their curse. Whatever its advantages or evils, and whatever the motivations of its defenders, slavery was at bottom a terrible problem long since bred into their society and intimately involved with its most vital parts. Like surgery, its excision by any means was certain to be both painful and dangerous, and there were no precedents to indicate with any certainty what the results would be. The Southerners of 1861 were the victims as well as the defenders of their peculiar institution.

The slaveholders who abhorred the worst practices of the system resented the implication that these were universal and sought increasingly to identify all that was good in Southern life with slavery. The non-slaveholding small farmers, small businessmen, teachers, preachers, clerks, lawyers, and white laborers, many of them desperately poor, who made up three-fourths of the Southern population knew only that the end of slavery could have calamitous possibilities. Some still aspired to be slaveholders. Countless others feared the economic and social competition of the slave. Many could be moved to terror by the picture of violence, chaos, and bloodshed conjured up by vote-hunting politicians. By 1861 they were ready to fight for a plantation type of civilization in which less than 3 per cent of the Southern people actually shared.

In politics Southern Democrats were Jeffersonian in outlook. They opposed the protective tariffs which raised the prices they must pay and reduced the markets for Southern crops abroad. They objected to federally financed internal improvements which might deplete the treasury and create a necessity for higher tariffs. They applauded Andrew Jackson's war on the United States Bank and distrusted the Northern banking and business community in general.

To make these economic issues a vital part of the sectional conflict, however, is to ignore the enormous strength of the Southern Whig party until the party was destroyed by the slavery quarrel in the 1850's. As Charles Sellers has shown, the Whig party in the slave states actually enjoyed a slight edge over the Democrats in both presidential and congressional elections in the 1830's and 1840's. Also, the Southern Whig congressmen on the whole supported the same commercial, industrial, and financial interests and policies as their Northern Whig colleagues. The antebellum South had its powerful urban commercial and banking interests too, and a majority of the great planters followed their lead in politics. The ancient myth of the South's provoking war and defeat by its united opposition to economic policies needed by Northern businessmen has lived too long. There were as many former Whigs, including Confederate Vice-President Alexander H. Stephens and Secretary of War Judah P. Benjamin, as there were Democrats in the ranks of secession in 1861.

In the end, however, the fiercely competing economic and political interests which had given the South a healthy two-party system and had kept the region in a lively turmoil for years finally formed a united front in defense of slavery and the right to extend it to new territories. No other issue could have achieved this result.

The Southwest differed in many ways from the Southeast, but in the end the common denominator of slavery drew them together as one section. The Northwest, however, remained in many ways distinct from the Northeast. The great region composed of Ohio, Indiana, Illinois, Wisconsin, and Michigan, and later Iowa and Minnesota, provided the spark of nationalism which held the Union together. In 1861 northeastern abolitionists like William Lloyd Garrison and Horace Greeley were willing for the erring Southern sisters to depart in peace. Abraham Lincoln of Illinois, however, speaking for his own section, could not allow the great American experiment in democracy to be split apart by secession.

The earliest settlers in the Northwest were largely Southerners. By 1830 there were nearly 700,000 former Southerners in the area, and they still equaled all other groups in 1850. Tens of thousands of Scotch-Irish, Welsh, and German frontiersmen had started from the great melting pot of western Pennsylvania and had briefly settled in North Carolina, Tennessee, Kentucky, and points even further south before slowly emigrating back northward into southern Ohio, Illinois, and Indiana. The Southerners believed that land that wouldn't grow trees wouldn't grow crops either, and as a result most of them picked land with trees and water. They ignored the rich but tough-sodded prairies and spent countless laborious hours chopping out the timber. The prairies were left for a later generation of New Englanders, who quickly invented adequate plows.

The Death of Slavery

These and other factors, including proximity to the South, tended to place Southerners on lands untouched by the glaciers, although forests also grew on unglaciated land. Frederick Jackson Turner once marked a map of the Northwest in different colors to show the glaciated and unglaciated land. He then marked with the same colors another map showing the areas which had voted for Abraham Lincoln and for Stephen A. Douglas in 1860. The patterns were almost identical. Lincoln the Kentuckian had moved to Illinois to become the hero of the New England element, while Douglas from New Hampshire had become the idol of the Illinois upland Southerners.

The Southern immigrants were mostly plain cabin people who loved to cut down trees, fired long rifles with rare skill, were often intemperate, and were still oftener illiterate. They enjoyed moving, and the covered wagon was always ready for loading at the word of better pickings in a new location. Some carried a few books and advocated education. Medical care was primitive, and death was omnipresent. Their folksongs and hymns, naturally enough, were frequently mournful sagas of family tragedy and hopes for future reunions in a better world. In their religion and in political attitudes they were often highly emotional.

In 1861 many of this group, particularly in the Ohio River valley, remained sympathetic to their Southern brethren. Still more, however, had but few kind memories of their former slaveholding competitors. Often intolerant toward the slaves and freed Negroes, they were also violently opposed to any extension of slavery, and they bitterly resented the possibility that an independent South might cut their river route to New Orleans.

After 1830 a new wave of immigration poured into the

There Were Sections

Northwest from the Northeast. Indeed, New England would have been almost stripped of its population except for the new European immigrants thronging the harbors. Fleeing from agricultural depressions and urban industrial problems, and seeking the new opportunities offered by a rich frontier, New Englanders and other northeasterners came out in Great Lakes steamers, in covered wagons, on horseback, and on foot. New England towns, with their town squares, Congregationalist churches, and little Yales and Harvards, sprang up everywhere, until western New York, northern Ohio, Indiana, and Illinois, and parts of Michigan and Wisconsin, became virtually a greater New England.

These travelers were generally concerned with education and a more intellectual brand of religion. New Englanders frequently moved in entire communities after drawing up Mayflower-type compacts which not only listed the rules of membership, but also emphasized their reasons for moving in religious terms. Many New Englanders considered the West a great heathen area to be rescued for God's kingdom, and glorified their own quest for a new fortune accordingly. Their sense of religious mission was a comfort in the midst of hardship and danger, and it developed easily into a strong sense of national mission later. Such people ultimately opposed slavery not only as unchristian and undemocratic, but also as a barrier to the achievement of God's plan for America.

A third varied population group was also important. Immigrants from England, Ireland, Germany, and Scandinavia came in large numbers to escape various ills in Europe. The generation which came after the unsuccessful European revolutions of 1848 added a group short in numbers, but long in quality and devotion to democratic principles. To those who had fled from oppression as well as famine, the very word slavery was anathema. The spirit of nationalism and a willingness to defend their new nation against those who would divide it settled upon the new Americans easily but firmly.

In areas where the different groups intermingled, the adjustment occasionally took time. Southerners who hung clothes on bushes and worried little about boundaries learned to live with New Englanders who used clotheslines and made careful surveys. In Wisconsin the New England puritans had to adjust their blue laws to the habits of Germans who liked beer and Beethoven on Sundays and Irishmen prepared for any amusement on any day. Yankee religion had to compete with the simpler fundamentalist beliefs of the frontier revivalists, and mixed congregations were occasionally treated to furious debates between hellfire-and-brimstone practitioners and their more restrained competitors and brethren.

Like the other sections, however, the Northwest had certain unifying features despite the infinite variety of its land and people. Although numerous towns were approaching the status of cities by 1861, and each town had its merchants and capitalists, the overwhelming majority of the people were small independent farmers. Farmers wanted land, and new population meant economic progress for everyone. The demand for cheap or free government land was, therefore, almost universal. Senator Thomas Hart Benton of the border state of Missouri spoke for Southwest and Northwest alike when he pronounced the right to own land a natural right—an obvious corollary to life, liberty, and the pursuit of happiness.

Westerners, likewise, had a virtual mania for internal improvements like roads, bridges, canals, river and lake channels, and harbors at federal expense. A convention at St. Louis in

There Were Sections

1840 defined the Mississippi River from its mouth to its source as an inland harbor, and argued that as such it should be cleared of snags and sandbars for its entire length. The northwestern states incurred huge debts for such purposes, and often had difficulty choosing between Benton's program for reducing the price of public land and Henry Clay's plan for maintaining prices while distributing the money thus collected to the states for internal improvements.

On the questions of tariffs and banking the Northwest was divided. Enough northwesterners joined with Southerners to pass the low tariff bills of 1846 and 1857, but others were furiously angry over certain provisions in both. In general, westerners everywhere wanted all the paper money and credit they could find anywhere. They rejoiced at the inflation which followed President Jackson's war on the United States Bank, but promptly deserted Jackson's hand-picked successor, Van Buren, when the latter sought to take the government entirely out of the banking business and adopted hard-money, deflationary policies in general.

Westerners everywhere liked the rugged personality of Andrew Jackson and the antiaristocratic democratic philosophy of equal opportunity preached by his followers. The hard money and laissez-faire economic principles of the Jacksonian inner circle were far less popular, however. In 1840, when the Whigs themselves went democratic with log cabins, hard cider, and the old soldier William Henry Harrison, westerners gleefully helped vote the Democrats out of office.

In the 1840's the Democrats recovered much of their old strength in the Northwest by becoming the party of territorial expansion. Also, just as the Whigs were becoming more democratic in outlook and image, northwestern Democrats like

31

The Death of Slavery

Stephen A. Douglas and others were becoming more and more Whiggish in their economic posture. By 1849 Democrats Douglas and Benton were vying with each other in demands that the federal government finance the building of the transcontinental railroads, and Douglas was later responsible for the initial appropriation for the Illinois Central Railroad.

By 1850, however, northwesterners had developed a powerful animosity towards the South and its peculiar institution. When President Polk chose to fight for Texas and California, but compromised on the boundary of Oregon, many westerners felt betrayed. The lower tariff of 1846 and the restoration of the independent treasury were unpopular with others. Polk's veto of river and harbor legislation, and subsequent vetoes of homestead laws by the "pro-Southern" Northern Presidents Pierce and Buchanan added to the picture.

Men who felt they were building a greater America and developing a continent for democracy and Christianity often came to identify their wishes and policies with God's will. Southern opposition was regarded as a barrier to human progress and the growth and well-being of America as ordained by the Almighty himself. Naturally enough, also, Southern perversity was attributed largely to the corrupting influence of slavery. In northwestern language "slavocracy" was more than a term to describe a group supporting an inhumane institution. It became the symbol for a decadent aristocracy blocking the efforts of men who did their own work to expand and develop America into the nation it should be. Men from states with laws excluding free Negroes from their borders became the most implacable foes of slavery, and were ready to believe any charge, however unjustified, that the South was plotting to

There Were Sections

force slavery upon areas further west and would not hesitate to impose it on free states also if given the opportunity.

There were sections in the America of 1860, but each section contained many diverse elements, and the usual generalizations about any section are subject to serious qualifications. Americans everywhere had much in common, and among their institutions only slavery was unique. The Southern farmer with one or two slaves or perhaps a family of slaves, however, had more in common with the Northern small farmer than he did with the great plantation owner. And, as John C. Calhoun was quick to point out, the Northern factory owner shared many of the employer problems of the planter. By 1860, however, the dominant Southern leadership considered the other sections a mortal threat escapable only by secession. And in the act of seceding the South did in fact become a mortal threat to the American Union, a national state for which the non-slave sections were prepared to fight and die.

III

"If the Republic Must Be Blotted Out..."

> If the State cannot survive the anti-slavery agitation, then let the State perish. If the Church must be cast down by the strugglings of humanity to be free, then let the church fall, . . . If the American Union cannot be maintained, except by immolating human freedom on the altar of tyranny, then let the American Union be consumed by a living thunderbolt, and no tear be shed over its ashes. If the Republic must be blotted out from the roll of nations, by proclaiming liberty to the captives, then let the Republic sink beneath the waves of oblivion, . . .
>
> WILLIAM LLOYD GARRISON

A budding Southern movement against slavery at the time of the American Revolution was checked by the inability of anti-slavery Southerners like Washington, Jefferson, and Randolph to imagine an acceptable alternative, and Eli Whitney's cotton gin soon gave the institution a new economic strength. Still, however, antislavery newspapers sprang up in several Southern cities, and strong minorities argued eloquently for abolition in the constitutional conventions of both Virginia and Tennessee. Likewise, the ill-fated American Colonization Society, which recognized the racial barrier to emancipation, began in the South. In 1822, however, the alleged attempt of Denmark Vesey, a talented South Carolina mulatto preacher, to plan an insurrection led to the hanging of Vesey and thirty-four followers. The Vesey conspiracy probably existed only in inflamed white imaginations, but Southerners everywhere were horrified. This fear was renewed in 1831, when Nat Turner led some Virginia slaves in a revolt which cost the lives of more than fifty persons. These events, plus the rising volume of antislavery criticism from the North, ended the Southern antislavery movements forever.

Southerners, however, who moved north and west by the hundreds of thousands, usually took with them a deep-seated hatred of slavery. The great majority sought freedom from the stultifying economic competition of slavery, and usually remained racists with no desire whatever to see Southern slaves free to come northward. Some, however, left because they could not bear living where they had to watch the evils of slavery and act as though they approved. Abolitionists like James G. Birney, Edward Coles, Levi Coffin, John Rankin, the Grimke sisters, the Dickey brothers, Samuel Crothers, Gideon Blackburn, William T. Allen, and James A. Thome—to name only a few—were all transplanted Southerners.

It was both natural and inevitable that an antislavery movement should sweep through the Northeast and spread to the Northwest in the 1830's and 1840's. It was an age of reform, and slavery was clearly the most flagrant violation of the

The Death of Slavery

Sermon on the Mount and the Declaration of Independence to be found in America. Also, it was far away and could be attacked with an impunity not always enjoyed when combating evils nearer at hand. New Englanders in bitter conflict with each other on local matters could share a common antipathy toward slavery. Indeed, some found antislavery a useful channel into which otherwise dangerous emotions could be harmlessly diverted. Local defenders of long hours and low wages in northeastern factories resented Southern opposition to their favorite economic programs in Congress and found it easy to tolerate and even share the attacks on Southern slavery.

The motivations and characteristics of the Northern abolitionists were varied and complex enough to provide later historians with a wealth of controversy. The abolitionists were heroes for decades until the terrible results of twentieth-century fanaticism brought a new regard for compromise and new analyses stressing the faults, inconsistencies, and intolerance of the abolitionists. They were a prime target for the revisionist historians, and many of the criticisms were valid. The civil rights struggle of the 1950's and 1960's, however, has brought a new regard for their work, at least in Northern intellectual circles.

It has been argued successively that the abolitionists were driven by only the purest Christian virtues; that because of neurotic tendencies induced by personal frustration, they were intolerant, humorless, and vituperative, and that they attacked slavery as a substitute for an unfair world; that they were really displaced middle-income aristocrats striking back at a world dominated by the new leaders of commerce, finance, and industry; and that in fact, most of them were successful, happy, well-adjusted persons. The fact that most of them were Whigs

"If the Republic Must Be Blotted Out . . ."

in opposition to the democracy of Andrew Jackson is also cited to show their lack of genuine humanitarian concern. Whether the truly effective center of abolition was the Northeast or the Old Northwest has also been ardently debated, while some have argued that the northwestern abolitionists were either transplanted New Englanders or derived their ideas from the same holy source of religious principle. Still others have gone a step backward to England to find the true origins of the movement.

Suffice to say that the evidence supports all of these contentions. Garrison was neurotic and spoke in the accents of hatred. John Brown was criminally insane. Parker, Phillips, Beecher, and Gerrit Smith were dedicated but wholly intolerant. Weld, the Grimke sisters, and many of the Quakers were genuinely humanitarian Christians; Tappan, Emerson, and Dana fretted at the onslaught of modern industrialism; fifty-nine of sixty Massachusetts abolitionists were Whigs; and Lowell, Whittier, and Longfellow were apparently supremely happy men. The personalities of the nameless thousands who followed them cannot be analyzed, but it may be assumed that the same variety ran entirely through the movement.

Whatever their character, the abolitionists were never more than a tiny minority of the whole people. Indeed, until well into the 1840's, most of them were proscribed by their own churches, even in New England. Moses Stuart, professor of Hebrew at Andover Theological Seminary, justified slavery from the Old Testament. President Lord of Dartmouth argued that slavery was an institution of God, and Episcopal Bishop Hopkins of Vermont was no less a fervent defender of slavery. Theodore Parker's colleagues would not exchange pulpits with him. The Methodist General Conference of 1838 censured two

37

The Death of Slavery

of its members who had spoken for abolition, and the New York Methodist Conference of the same year warned its members not to read the antislavery paper *Zion's Watchman*. By 1850 the abolition societies claimed a total membership of 150,000, but those members active enough to be remembered number fewer than 250.

The abolitionist who had the greatest sustained impact upon the South was clearly William Lloyd Garrison, whose rabid demands for immediate emancipation regardless of the cost won but few Northern followers. Abandoned by a drunken father and condemned to a miserable childhood, Garrison reached manhood steeped in anger at an unfair and unjust world. After a harsh apprenticeship as a printer and writer, Garrison finally became editor of the *National Philanthropist*, a newspaper dedicated to the suppression of intemperance and other vices of the less godly. Editor Garrison soon added lotteries, sabbath-breaking, and war to his list of enemies. Then he was invited to help Benjamin Lundy edit an abolition paper in Baltimore. At Jonesboro, Tennessee, Lundy had earlier published one of America's earliest abolition papers. In Baltimore Garrison was jailed and mistreated.

Overnight Garrison abandoned gradual emancipation and called for abolition immediately and by force and violence if necessary. In 1830 he founded *The Liberator* in Boston and announced: *"I do not wish to think or speak or write with moderation. I will not retreat a single inch, and I will be heard."* To Garrison the problem was a simple one of right and wrong. Slavery violated Christianity and the Declaration of Independence. If the Constitution protected slavery, then this "League with Death and agreement with Hell" should be destroyed, and Garrison illustrated his point by burning a copy of the Constitution over a candle while his audience breathed a fervent

"Amen." To Garrison slaveholders were no better than criminals and deserved no protection or consideration whatever. Slavery must be abolished regardless of any cost in bloodshed and suffering.

Small wonder that Southerners, whether slaveholders or not, were frightened by the doctrines of Garrison, and small wonder that Garrison's Northern following was never very numerous. The circulation of *The Liberator* was never more than three thousand, but Southern editors regularly reprinted his insults and attacks.

Southern policies of the immediate antebellum period were clearly dictated by fear, pride, and emotion rather than a rational calculation of self-interest, and much of the responsibility for this must be laid to Garrison. In the end he helped frighten the South into self-destructive actions far more dangerous to the South and to slavery than any actions seriously contemplated by either the leaders or the people of the Northern states. With the possible exception of John Brown, no one ever quite equaled the position of Garrison in Southern minds as the stereotype example of the Yankee enemy.

The man who did the most to make abolition respectable and who won by far the most converts was Theodore Dwight Weld. Weld preached gradual emancipation, to begin immediately and to be accomplished within the existing constitutional and political framework. Weld's program did not suggest war and bloodshed, and did not threaten or heap abuse upon the state, the church, or the white Southerners. Although Garrison ultimately adopted a pacifist philosophy which excused him from direct action of any sort, he established his reputation with the loudly proclaimed principle that the end justified any means. Weld preached no such doctrine.

Converted to religion by the great Christian Perfectionist,

The Death of Slavery

Charles G. Finney, Weld became an abolitionist on the basis of Christian principle. By 1832 he was a somewhat mature student at Lane Theological Seminary in Cincinnati, where he organized a series of debates on the twin subjects of abolition and colonization.

The president of Lane was Lyman Beecher, a well-known New England theologian. Beecher's daughter Harriet was destined to write *Uncle Tom's Cabin,* and his son Henry Ward would become an abolitionist after whom frontier Free Soilers would name their rifles "Beecher's Bibles."

In 1832, however, the elder Beecher was far less bold. He bowed to local pressures and ordered the debates stopped even though abolitionists were among the institution's chief contributors. More than fifty students led by Weld resigned, and most of them ultimately moved northward to Oberlin, a small church college founded the year before by John T. Shipherd and Philo Stewart. Under the influence of Asa Mahan, John Morgan, Weld, and Finney, and with financial aid from men like Arthur Tappan, Oberlin became a great radiating center of Christian Perfectionism, social reform, and abolitionism. Among the institution's earliest heresies was the admission of both Negroes and women to full academic equality, and its tradition of academic freedom remains unsurpassed. As might have been expected, the college also became an important station on the Underground Railroad.

With Oberlin as one of his bases, Weld in good biblical fashion trained seventy disciples to go forth and spread the gospel of God's objections to slavery. At first the seventy were suppressed, insulted, and occasionally manhandled. On March 3, 1837, a young Illinois legislator named Abraham Lincoln expressed a widely held view: "The institution of slavery is

40

"If the Republic Must Be Blotted Out . . ."

founded on both injustice and bad policy, but . . . the promulgation of abolition doctrines tends rather to increase than abate its evils." By peaceful but dedicated perseverance, however, Weld's apostles slowly won forbearance and then respect.

Meanwhile, Weld joined Garrison, the Tappan brothers, and others in the American Anti-Slavery Society. The society printed and circulated antislavery tracts by the thousands, while Weld and his group took the lead in gathering thousands of signatures for petitions asking Congress to abolish slavery in the District of Columbia. If gradual emancipation were to begin immediately, where better than in the District, where Congress was the only government and where no state laws protecting slavery existed?

The petition movement was a stroke of genius. At this point the abolitionists were still a tiny group generally regarded as crackpots. The struggle in Congress over the petitions, however, gave their movement a new base and a new appeal. The sacred right of petition could not be threatened without rousing the anger of Americans almost everywhere. Yet the South's most prominent leader found a resistance to the right of petition itself to be politically expedient. Weld and his great supporter, John Quincy Adams, found an inadvertent ally in John C. Calhoun, but this cannot be fully understood without a close look at the politics of the young American nation.

IV

Democracy and Its Leaders

By the mid-1830's American politicians had developed a new set of motivations, and were becoming more and more aware of the value of emotional appeals often unrelated to genuine issues.

Jacksonian Democracy had come to America in the wake of an ever-expanding electorate, and it had brought with it the principle of giving the jobs and favors to the faithful of the victorious party. As government grew in size at every level from town council to the federal executive departments, elections became more and more important to more and more people for reasons often unrelated to contending principles and national policies. The competition for power and influence remained for some a struggle between philosophies and programs. For some it also became an economic profession. For still others it became a gigantic sport with prestige, power, and the sheer joy of victory as the rewards. For all too many, issues had become weapons to be sought out, managed, and utilized in the endless quest for votes among the body politic.

In short, the United States had achieved a democracy ideally suited for reasonably wise and just decision-making where none of the alternatives posed any mortal threat to the real or imagined interests of any particular group or section. The system was also destined to function magnificently even in crises threatening the very existence of the Republic when the major problem was an easily identified external enemy. But it was not a system designed to handle peacefully a question like slavery unless the political leadership on both sides should rise above the temptations offered by such an issue.

If politics was a full-time profession for many, it was a major participation sport for almost everyone. Americans were a competitive people, and the almost continuous political contests filled a void to be crammed to overflowing in later years by radio, television, movies, and nationally organized athletics. In taverns, inns, hotels, stores, blacksmith shops, and courthouses—indeed, anywhere men could be found—Americans argued and quarreled incessantly over candidates and issues. European travelers were astounded at the vigorous arguments and assumption of absolute knowledge of the widest variety of political subjects by unlettered citizens in every village, hamlet, and farmhouse.

The fountains of knowledge were the local newspapers and a handful of papers and magazines national in scope, almost all of which were openly allied with one political party or the other and often with one leader or faction of that party. Editors exchanged subscriptions and copied, supported, and disputed each others' news and views. National papers like the Demo-

The Death of Slavery

cratic *Washington Globe* and *New York Evening Post* and the Whig *National Intelligencer, Chicago Tribune,* and *New York Tribune* fed news and editorials to their satellites in the same fashion as a modern press service. Although large sections of the proceedings in Congress were reported verbatim, most editors saw fit to minimize or limit what Francis P. Blair called "the stale and worn-out speeches" of the opposition. Both the *Globe* and the *Intelligencer* printed and distributed by the thousands the more effective speeches of their favorite leaders. Copies of newspapers and magazines circulated from hand to hand and were read by far more people than their subscription lists would indicate.

An unfortunate accompaniment of this essentially healthy interest in politics was an addiction to violence in many parts of the country. A people who had spent so many years shooting Indians and animals and who had written the right of every individual to bear arms into their national Constitution found violent personal conflicts easy to forgive if the antagonists had a theoretically even chance to kill or maim each other. Judges and juries alike were remarkably lenient to the victors of fatal encounters, and in numerous states dueling itself was still legal.

While criminal violence abounded in the poorer areas of the great northeastern cities, it was primarily in the South and West that both politicians and editors found their professions dangerous. Andrew Jackson carried a varied assortment of lead in his thin, weary body. Thomas Hart Benton, in addition to his pistol fight with Jackson, had killed a man in a duel at nine feet, with this point-blank distance set by Benton to offset a complaint that his marksmanship was superior. Representative Spencer Pettis and Major Thomas Biddle, brother of Nicholas Biddle, killed each other in a five-foot duel, with this suicidal

Democracy and Its Leaders

range set by Biddle to compensate for his nearsightedness. Representative Cilley of Maine was killed by Representative Graves of Kentucky in a rifle duel which Cilley had done his best to avoid. Happily, a duel between Henry Clay and John Randolph ended harmlessly. Daniel Webster was intelligent enough to refuse a challenge from Randolph and fortunate to represent a state which put no premium on recklessness or marksmanship. Sam Houston gave his congressional colleague Stansberry a frightful thrashing on a Washington street. Editor Francis P. Blair carried a pistol and avoided duels in part because of his reputation for marksmanship. Blair's competitor Duff Green, who worshiped at the Calhoun shrine, did fight duels and once received a terrible beating at the hands of South Carolina unionist James Blair. In Frankfort, Kentucky, editor Thomas Benning was killed in cold blood by Charles Wickliffe, who was himself later killed in a duel by Benning's successor. Editor J. H. Pleasants of Richmond, who once threatened Francis P. Blair, was killed by Thomas Ritchie, Jr., son of Pleasants' rival editor in Richmond. Accounts of such incidents could be multiplied many times.

Obviously, the great majority of politicians and editors did not get involved in mayhem, but the public tolerance of violence was probably an important factor in the coming of the American Civil War. The all too frequent translation of political disagreement and rivalry into personal hatred and physical conflict made the realistic appraisal of emotional issues more difficult. A traditional indifference to violence also helped keep both Southerners and Northerners unaware of the frightful extremities a military solution of their difficulties would reach. Southerners really believed their boast that any of their number could whip ten Yankees, and this notion contributed not a little to their incredibly light-hearted and optimistic approach to the question of war.

The politician who used the slavery issue most consistently if not always most effectively for his own ends was John C. Calhoun of South Carolina. Puritanical, humorless, and self-righteous, Calhoun usually translated his own ambitions and problems into matters of universal significance, and he commanded a fanatical devotion among his followers. Calhoun has fascinated and won high praise from the historians of the South and the North alike, and his place in history has grown in importance from the American tendency to view the heroes of lost causes with feelings of sportsmanlike sympathy. Only when his most cherished premises are examined in minute detail and when the full scale of twists and turns in his career is traced do cracks in the traditional Calhoun image begin to appear.

In 1812 the young Calhoun was a war hawk determined to punish Britain and liberate Canada. In succeeding years he was a great nationalist and supported both the protective tariff and the United States Bank. As Secretary of War under President Monroe, Calhoun was one of the five candidates for President in 1824 and accepted the vice-presidency in the runoff between Jackson and Adams. In 1828 he again accepted the second place after apparently being persuaded that the ailing Andrew Jackson could last but one term at best.

In 1828 Calhoun was certain he would be the next President, but his path to the White House was suddenly blocked by unforeseen circumstances. Old Hickory's beloved wife Rachel had died, reportedly from shock caused by the vicious and untrue stories circulated during the campaign about the circumstances of her marriage to Jackson. Unable to save Rachel and heartbroken by her death, Jackson arrived in Washington just in time to discover a similar situation involving his new Secretary of War, John Eaton. Eaton had married a young widow of questionable repute, and the other administration wives, at least partly from jealousy of her good looks, were soon pointedly ignoring her parties and not inviting her to theirs. There is evidence also that pro-Calhoun men in the cabinet hoped thereby to drive Eaton out because Eaton was one of the few cabinet members devoted to Calhoun's chief rival for the succession, Secretary of State Martin Van Buren.

Andrew Jackson promptly made Mrs. Eaton's cause his own and pronounced her "pure as the driven snow." In this squabble, the aristocratic Mrs. Calhoun was ostentatiously on the side of Mrs. Eaton's enemies, while Van Buren, a widower, was free to attend Mrs. Eaton publicly and spend long hours with his fellow widower, Jackson, in conversations about the wickedness of female gossip.

Also, when Calhoun's friends, including Duff Green, editor of the administration newspaper, began to push the Carolinian's claims for a presidential nomination in 1832, Van Buren's friends realized that the iron-willed Jackson would live through another term and longer if he so decided. Soon they produced correspondence which showed that Calhoun as Secretary of War had suggested a court-martial for Jackson at the time of Old Hickory's invasion of Florida in 1818. Already angered by the Eaton affair, Jackson demanded an explanation which Calhoun could not provide, and their break was complete. Calhoun resigned from the vice-presidency and returned to South Carolina to be elected to the Senate.

Finding himself in open conflict with Jackson, the full extent of whose invincible popularity was not yet fully clear in 1830,

The Death of Slavery

Calhoun turned to South Carolina and the other Southern states for a new political base. In 1828 he had already penned anonymously his doctrine of nullification because of South Carolina's anger over the tariff. In this document he had argued persuasively that ultimate sovereignty rested in the states rather than in the federal government, and that any state could declare federal laws unconstitutional and refuse to obey them. If three-fourths of the states, meeting in conventions, should rule the law in question constitutional, it would indeed be so, inasmuch as three-fourths of the states have the power to amend the Constitution. Otherwise, however, the disobedience or "nullification" should stand. Even if three-fourths of the states should make the law valid, the nullifying state should still have a choice between submission and secession.

Nullification was directed against the tariff. Andrew Jackson was personally a low tariff man and a slaveholding Southern planter, and his land policies were calculated to fill the treasury and render the high tariff both unnecessary and inexpedient. Henry Clay was virtually the father of the protective tariff, but in the election of 1832 Calhoun and his friends gave their unqualified support to Clay. Jackson's election, said Duff Green's *Telegraph*, would enable "daring and corrupt politicians" to "subvert the very foundations of liberty, and convert this government into the corrupt engine of the most odious and profligate despotism."

In 1832 Americans elected a Congress which by all contemporary accounts was low tariff in sentiment. The horse and water transportation of those years, however, dictated that the Congress chosen in 1832 would not take office until December, 1833. The other low tariff states were prepared to wait calmly for a peaceful solution in their favor, but Calhoun was unwilling to see the issue settled so easily. Congress met in December, 1832, to receive the stern announcement by President Jackson that South Carolina was attempting to disobey a federal law. A substantial naval force was already en route to Charleston, and Congress was soon debating an authorization for the use of force, which Old Hickory clearly intended to use whether the bill passed or not. In the end the crisis was resolved with a compromise tariff which provided for a gradual reduction of the tariff over a ten year period to a 20 per cent level and thereby put the question off limits for succeeding Congresses until 1842. For the rest of his life Henry Clay credited Calhoun with saving the tariff in 1833.

The compromise was hardly a Southern victory. The act of 1832 had eliminated the tariff on the cheap woolens worn by almost all Southern slaves. The compromise tariff of 1833 restored this duty to 50 per cent and also provided for evaluations at the port of entry rather than the port of departure—a provision which added the cost of transportation to the base value for taxation.

The best hope for the high tariff was the possibility that the national treasury could be emptied by 1842, since low tariffs were the natural product of a full treasury. In 1835, however, Calhoun originated a program for giving the surplus funds from the national treasury to the states. In 1836 this plan became law in the guise of a "deposit" bill which decreed that the money was to be returnable immediately upon demand. The states received and quickly spent more than $23,000,000, and the federal government still has a lien against the states that spent it. This venture and some other mishaps reduced the $36,000,000 surplus of 1836 to a deficit of $12,000,000 by the end of 1837. A new revenue tariff was absolutely essential by 1842.

The Death of Slavery

Having opposed the Democratic administration as long as it was headed by the slaveholding Tennessee planter, Calhoun promptly rejoined his old party when Jackson was replaced by the essentially far more libertarian New Yorker, Martin Van Buren. With no visible pain, Calhoun switched from support of the United States Bank to advocating the independent treasury program of Van Buren, and he joined his old enemy Thomas Hart Benton in stopping the final treasury payment to the states.

After Van Buren's defeat in 1840, Calhoun saw more new light. After an internal improvements convention at Memphis he discovered that the Mississippi river was "a great inland sea," and began to advocate internal improvements at federal expense. He also promised northeastern industrialists that he would support a tariff in exchange for their help in reaching the White House, and he reiterated his earlier arguments that employers of free and slave labor alike should be united against any show of independence by their workers. Northeastern industrialists and Southern planters should stand together against the common enemy, said Calhoun, because men who worked with their hands, whether white or black, slave or free, had neither the capacity for nor the right to equality or liberty. Slavery, said Calhoun, was "the most safe and stable basis for free institutions in the world. It is impossible with us that conflict can take place between labor and capital which makes it so difficult to establish and maintain free institutions throughout the wealthy and highly civilized nations where such institutions as ours do not exist."

When antislavery pamphlets appeared in the Southern mails in 1835, Calhoun demanded unsuccessfully that Congress forbid their delivery. When the petitions for abolition in the District began to flood Congress, most of the members urged that the petitions be accepted and promptly tabled without discussion. Calhoun, however, insisted that the petitions be rejected to show that Congress had no constitutional power on the subject. The result was the first congressional debate over slavery, a debate in which the abolitionists were pushed by Calhoun into the highly respectable role of defenders of the sacred right of petition. Almost alone, Calhoun turned the petitions into a major issue and set about to project further his own image as the South's great defender against those who would destroy his version of the only true democracy.

Henry Clay was almost the antithesis of Calhoun. Correctly described by enemies as the "victor of many a well-fought bottle," admittedly an almost compulsive gambler at cards, and with an attractiveness for women which inspired much gossip, Clay was widely loved by a public which would never elect him President. A slaveholder who considered slavery evil, Clay was a leader in the African colonization movement. Knowing his own weaknesses, Clay easily forgave the sins of others. His role as the Great Pacificator in the sectional quarrel was well-earned.

Like Calhoun, Clay detested Andrew Jackson, but unlike Calhoun, Clay kept his views clear and consistent. He spent a lifetime working for an America in which a strong and paternalistic central government would promote economic growth through protective tariffs, a national bank, an adequate paper money system, and federal financing of roads, canals, river and harbor channels, and other such internal improvements. He hoped that slavery would some day disappear but prayed that any attempted solution of the issue would be delayed as long as possible.

The Death of Slavery

Daniel Webster of Massachusetts shared Clay's economic views both on principle and from personal interest. He was a heavy investor in factories and a highly paid attorney for the Bank of the United States. Magnificent in appearance and with a superb voice and command of words, Webster was established by the mid-1830's as the great orator of nationalism. He had been a states' rights adovcate at the Hartford Convention of 1815, and had opposed the tariff and the Bank in 1816 and 1817. As New England turned to manufacturing, however, Webster by 1824 was answering brilliantly all his own earlier arguments. As Southerners opposed the tariff in the name of states' rights, Webster found nationalism a powerful emotional instrument for use in rebuttal. In phrases unmatched before or since, except possibly by Lincoln's Gettysburg Address, Webster held aloft a vision of the great and indissoluble American Union which set fire to men's hearts everywhere. Like many men, Webster was captivated by his own arguments and became totally dedicated to a role perhaps begun originally on a note of sophistry. Fate played cruel tricks on Daniel Webster. For the presidency he was always a step behind Clay as a candidate because Clay had wider popular support. In 1840 and 1848, however, Webster haughtily refused nominations for Vice-President. These were the only two elections won by his party in its history, and in each case the President was soon stricken with a fatal illness.

Just as dedicated to the Union as Webster and Clay was their lifelong opponent, Thomas Hart Benton of Missouri. Benton was a strange blend of Southern agrarian economics and western vision. In one breath he would astound listeners with predictions of a future continental America of 160,000,000 people bound together by steam cars racing at 100 miles an hour across the prairies and plains, and in the next he would insist upon the abolition of all paper money except large bills. Even before Webster and Lincoln he was preaching the concept of the United States as a great universal experiment in democracy destined to change the course of human events throughout the world.

Although Benton had exchanged shots with Andrew Jackson, by the 1830's the two had long since been reconciled and Benton had become a worshiper at the Jackson shrine. He was the acknowledged senatorial spokesman and administration leader for both Jackson and Van Buren.

From a combination of personal and political considerations and genuine conviction, Benton in 1832 began denouncing Calhoun as an enemy of the Union. He saw first the tariff issue and then the slavery question as problems which the Carolinian was deliberately exaggerating and distorting for the sake of political ambitions. Like Clay and Webster, Benton hoped and believed that time, economic disadvantage, and perhaps the hand of Providence would eventually enable the United States to eliminate slavery without bloodshed. He was certain also that the racial difference was the only serious obstacle to an ultimately peaceful solution. Benton condemned the abolitionists as foolish incendiaries who were in reality hurting the cause they were promoting, but he reserved his bitterest attacks for those Southerners like Calhoun who in his opinion were playing directly into the hands of the abolitionists.

In his speeches over a thirty-year period and in his two-volume *Thirty Years View*, completed in 1856, Benton offered in advance the first of the modern revisionist views of the coming of the Civil War. The abolitionists and the Southern fire-eaters, he wrote, were the two blades of a pair of scissors.

The Death of Slavery

Alone neither could harm the Union; together, if unchecked, they would cut it in half. Benton's view of his own "blundering generation" differed occasionally in the selection of the "blunderers" from that of James Randall some ninety years later, but the general thesis was the same. Similarly, the exaggerations and distortions described by Avery Craven and Allan Nevins in the 1940's were nowhere discussed with greater contemporary understanding than in the words of Benton.

Benton's views were shared by his friend, Francis Preston Blair, editor of the Jacksonian newspaper, the *Globe*. "The Nullifiers," wrote Blair in 1835, "are far more numerous and talented than the Abolitionists. They give a striking proof of their superior adroitness, in the use they make of their rivals in the evil work of disunion." As Jackson's personal editor and chief dispenser of administration ideas and principles to some four hundred other Democratic papers, Blair was a powerful force in the Jackson and Van Buren administrations. Blair dramatized in stirring language the philosophy of Jacksonian democracy and contributed directly to much of the nation's reforming spirit. Until the 1850's, however, he sharply opposed the abolitionists, and saw no inconsistency in this opposition.

The ancient patriarchs and bitter enemies, Andrew Jackson and John Quincy Adams, remained influential well into the 1840's. The indomitable Jackson returned to his Hermitage plantation near Nashville, Tennessee. Still possessed of great popular appeal, the old man kept his place in the hearts of disciples on the political stage. A benevolent slaveholder, Jackson abhorred the abolitionists, but he was never able to take them very seriously as a genuine threat to the South.

Adams had become President in 1824 and was magnificently equipped for the position in every respect but two. He had knowledge, ability, dedication, and vision, but he did not project a warm or colorful image, and he was unwilling to be a politician. He refused to fire his enemies, hire his friends, or use his powerful office in any way to win loyal supporters and workers. His dreams, plans, and programs were systematically frustrated by Congress, and he suffered a humiliating defeat at the hands of the backwoods general, Andrew Jackson, in 1828.

By the late 1830's, Adams, still somewhat bitter and cynical but as independent-minded as ever, was back in Washington as a representative. He was an abolitionist primarily because he recognized the unhappy impact of the institution on the nation as a whole, and the petitions against slavery in the District of Columbia won his immediate support. With Theodore Dwight Weld as an adviser, Adams year in and year out defended the right of the petitioners to have their plea heard. His speeches won him the sobriquet Old Man Eloquent from supporters, but many less complimentary titles from others. In defending the right of petition on principle, Adams at one point sought unsuccessfully to introduce a petition from certain citizens calling for a breakup of the American Union. His purpose was clear to the sophisticated observer, but appeared little short of treason in the Democratic presses. The right of petition was a holy principle for many Americans, however, and the alliance of Adams and the abolitionists for its defense greatly increased the respectability of abolitionism in many northern communities.

Martin Van Buren, Jackson's heir apparent, became President in 1836. Van Buren's career, wrote William Cullen Bryant, had been "one of unobtrusive usefulness, not of turbulent injury." "Little Van" was loved by fierce partisans like Jackson, Benton, and Blair, but he was very different from them in personality.

The Death of Slavery

He was a man of sophistication and humility who lacked his friends' capacity to reduce political issues to struggles between light and darkness. He found the role of a warrior politician an impossible pose, and no amount of *Globe* rhetoric could make him a second Jackson.

Extensive wildcat banking and a flood of banknotes supported by their acceptability as payment for public lands had brought a great boom in land sales and business expansion. Fearing the rising inflation and unable to persuade Congress to check the bubble, Jackson in 1836 had the Treasury issue a "specie circular," requiring hard money for public lands. Overnight millions of dollars in banknotes became worthless and many local banks collapsed. Meanwhile, the banks in which Jackson had placed the national treasury had loaned out much of it before the deposit bill of Calhoun and Clay required them to transfer the federal funds to the states. This ruined many of these banks, and two successive years of American crop failures and a tightening of credit in Europe completed the picture. The prosperous America which had elected Van Buren became overnight an unhappy land of unemployment, bankruptcies, business failures, and foreclosures.

Jackson had ruled a Democratic party badly divided, but held together by Old Hickory's power at the ballot box and the advantages of membership in a victorious party. Van Buren had no such magic, and the depression left him open to attack from every direction.

Van Buren blamed the national banking system which had caused the inflationary boom in the first place. He was compelled to issue treasury notes to keep the government afloat, but his permanent solution was the creation of a new independent treasury which would keep and disburse government funds, and be entirely unconnected with either banking or paper money. The program finally passed Congress in 1840, but not before it had caused angry divisions in the Democratic party.

The small group who had been closest to Andrew Jackson—men like Van Buren, Blair, Benton, Polk, Taney, and Wright—were democrats in political philosophy, but conservative on economic questions. In ringing phrases they called for greater equality of opportunity for all Americans to share in the nation's wealth and power. Simultaneously, except for Indian removal and cheap land, they opposed banking, tariff, currency, and internal improvements programs designed to enlist the federal government in the movement to create more total wealth for Americans to share. Men who had risen to great power by preaching democracy found their most cherished economic principles threatened by the very hopes and ambitions they had done so much to stimulate. Even in the days of Jackson, significant numbers of nominal Democrats had supported Whig policies, and Old Hickory's most important victories had come through his use of the veto. Democrats had overwhelmingly supported the deposit act whereas only a handful had favored Jackson's specie circular.

In 1840 the Whigs took full advantage of the recent though fading depression, divisions among the Democrats, and the unspectacular image of President Van Buren. They nominated William Henry Harrison, the ancient hero of Tippecanoe. They adopted no platform and forbade Harrison to utter a word on any issue. In a series of speeches and pamphlets they produced a devastating collection of falsehoods about Van Buren. The President was pictured as a "sweet sandy-whiskered," overfed eastern aristocrat, who pranced about in corsets, spent much time before the mirror, wasted immense sums of public money on personal luxuries, and ate nothing but gourmet delicacies off golden plates. Even the installation of a bathtub in the White House became a major crime. Harrison in contrast was a rough-and-ready hero who had fought Indians and the British and was possessed of all the homely virtues of the frontier and the farm. Harrison was the candidate who would be content with a log cabin, plenty of hard cider, and an occasional cold shower or dip in the creek. In vain did the Democrats point out that only one wing of the Harrison mansion had any logs in it and challenge the candidate to take a stand on significant issues.

Harrison's Whig followers included both abolitionists and slaveholders, but the latter were at least partially mollified by the selection of John Tyler of Virginia as the vice-presidential running mate. Democrats tried to make an issue of Harrison's onetime membership in an abolition society, but the Whigs countered with a more recent event. An obscure naval officer was convicted of extreme cruelty on the evidence of a large number of white sailors and three Negroes. When Van Buren accepted the verdict of the court-martial, which had also been approved by all subordinate authorities, the Whigs flooded the South with pamphlets accusing the President of accepting Negro testimony against a white officer.

In the end Harrison was elected, and American politicians had learned some new lessons in the art of gaining votes. The new President, however, already ailing in body and spirit, found the constant badgering and pleading of his followers for political appointments almost unendurable. From a variety of causes, including the job itself, Harrison died only a month after taking office.

With Whig majorities in Congress, leaders like Clay and

Democracy and Its Leaders

Webster returned to Washington determined to undo all the wicked works of Andrew Jackson and get America again on the road to their "American system." They were not prepared, however, for John Tyler. Finding himself unexpectedly in the White House, Tyler promptly reverted to the principles of a states' rights Virginia planter. The Whigs voted the independent treasury out of existence and twice passed laws chartering a new national bank. Each time President Tyler vetoed this central policy of his adopted party. The tariff likewise met the same fate until a destitute treasury compelled him to accept a set of moderate duties in 1842. The Whigs passed Clay's program for distributing the proceeds of federal land sales to the states for internal improvements, but even this was eliminated by a rider declaring it void if tariffs should rise above 20 per cent. By 1843 Clay had resigned from the Senate, all of Tyler's cabinet except Webster had resigned, and the Whig party was in chaos, its splendid victory of 1840 turned to ashes by the obstinacy of John Tyler.

As the Whigs continued to thrash about in their own web, the Democratic presidential nomination for 1844 glittered ever more brightly. With no Jackson or any other dominant personality in sight, the stage was set for America's first real intraparty fight for a party nomination. The raucous, gamelike election of 1840 had avoided the significant problems. That of 1844 would create issues destined to plague Americans for a generation.

V

"If the Union Is to Break..."

In 1844 personal ambitions and bitter rivalries of long standing, a major national issue, and a Presidential election combined to generate new sectional quarrels and link them irrevocably with America's inevitable march to the Pacific.

Although Henry Clay was the only obvious Whig candidate for President, the Democratic party of 1843 had a surplus of would-be men of destiny.

Martin Van Buren, clearly a victim of inexcusable chicanery in 1840, hoped for vindication. Indeed, the renomination of Van Buren in 1844 had become an obsession with ideological Jacksonians like Blair, Benton, and Silas Wright. The ability of ordinary people to vote intelligently was an essential part of the Jacksonian faith, but in 1840 Americans had responded to the crudest emotional appeals and had elected Harrison with no knowledge of his principles. To the Jacksonians this was a blow against democracy itself, and American voters had to be given a chance to vindicate themselves by electing Van Buren in 1844.

Northwesterners disenchanted with Jacksonian economic policies were far less enthusiastic about another effort for Van Buren. Governor Cass of Michigan was available, as was James Buchanan of Pennsylvania. Former Vice-President Richard M. Johnson also stood ready for the call. Johnson had supposedly slain the Indian chief Tecumseh at the Battle of the Thames in 1813, and this achievement plus a reputation for sympathy with industrial workers had brought him to the political heights despite an unorthodox personal life which included illegitimate daughters by his mulatto housekeeper.

Many Southern Democrats still dreamed of seeing Calhoun in the White House, and the Carolinian, having regained his Democratic status in the service of Van Buren, was still hopeful. Other nominal Democrats, having received recent favors from the President, were even advancing the claims of John Tyler because of his vetoes of key Whig policies. By the end of 1843 numerous public meetings, public letters, and editorials were expounding the virtues of each candidate.

Van Buren's opponents won their first victory by getting the convention scheduled for May, 1844, instead of the preceding fall or winter. Otherwise Van Buren would have been nominated. Although the little New Yorker lacked the Jackson aura of invincibility, many Democratic officeholders owed their jobs to him, and his prestige as an ex-President remained strong among local party workers. In state convention after state convention resolutions were passed pledging the delegations to his support.

Discouraged but not ready to surrender, the friends of both Tyler and Calhoun, meanwhile, found an issue whereby to

The Death of Slavery

dramatize their candidates. Texas had been a prominent question for seven years. In 1843 it suddenly became an overwhelming problem.

Texas had been settled by American frontiersmen attracted by the promise of 640 acres at twelve and one-half cents an acre. The Mexican government had invited them, allowed them to bring slavery despite Mexican laws against it, and given them full citizenship.

The political instability of Mexico and the differences in background and outlook, however, brought almost immediate trouble. The Texans were tough, acquisitive, energetic, and aggressive both with each other and with others. The Mexicans enjoyed afternoon siestas and did not feel that fortunes and empires had to be built every day. To the Texans the Mexicans appeared lazy, shiftless, and untrustworthy. Many Mexicans felt that the Yankees rushed through life so fast that they ran by more than they caught. There were also specific grievances. In 1830 Mexico passed laws forbidding further emigration to Texas and abolishing slavery. The Texans protested unsuccessfully in petitions and memorials, and Stephen Austin spent eight months in prison after delivering the resolutions of a Texas convention. By 1835 the revolution was in full swing. Americans were horrified to learn of the massacres at the Alamo and at Goliad, and there was widespread rejoicing in the United States when General Sam Houston defeated Santa Anna at San Jacinto in 1836 and thereby liberated Texas.

In Washington the United States Senate debated long and hard before recognizing the new Republic of Texas. Abolitionists protested that the affair was a slave plot to extend the wicked institution, and Benjamin Lundy published a pamphlet which required little reading beyond the title page: *The War*

"If the Union Is to Break . . ."

in Texas: A Review of Facts and Circumstances Showing That This Contest Is a Result of a Long and Premeditated Crusade against the Government Set on Foot by Slave Holders, and Perpetuating the System of Slavery and Slave Trade in the Republic of Mexico. In the Senate various moderates assailed the Lundy position and defended the Texans. "It may as well be said that our revolution was a war for the extension of slavery," said Thomas Hart Benton. "No revolt, not even our own, ever had a more just and a more sacred origin." Calhoun, however, insisted that the abolitionists were in fact correct. Texas, he said, should not only be recognized, but should be immediately annexed openly for the purpose of preserving and extending slavery. The North, insisted Calhoun, had a duty to annex Texas as a show of good faith and goodwill toward the South. The senate voted to recognize, but not to annex.

In 1837 President Van Buren declined a Texas petition for annexation on the ground that this would mean annexing a war with Mexico. In 1842 Tyler took the same position because of the opposition of Secretary of State Daniel Webster. Most Americans, leaders and people alike, apparently looked upon Texas as a fruit still green, but to be easily plucked as soon as it ripened. The American trade with Mexico was extensive and valuable, and there appeared to be no reason for a costly and perhaps bloody premature consummation of the inevitable union.

In the background, meanwhile, certain forces were working as a catalyst. Texas had issued more than $7,500,000 worth of bonds, which by 1841 had passed largely into the hands of well-placed Americans who had bought them for much less than their original value. Simultaneously, Texas had issued land warrants for many millions of acres, and many of these were

63

soon acquired by American speculators waiting for the rise. Money for propaganda urging the annexation of Texas was not difficult to obtain.

In 1843 the impatient President Houston began to combine feigned indifference toward the United States with well-publicized friendly personal relations with the British chargé d'affaires, Captain Charles Elliott. Elliott had just been recalled from Canton for losing a battle of wits to a Chinese viceroy. The Chinese had destroyed some twenty thousand chests of illegal British opium, a mistake for which the *Times* pronounced Elliott "notoriously unfit to manage a respectable apple stall." Anxious to retrieve his reputation, Elliott suggested a plan for Britain to provide Texas with a large loan and free trade in exchange for the abolition of Texas slavery.

Various British editors had already discussed the commercial advantages to British cotton and sugar colonies if Texas and, indeed, the entire American South should abandon slavery, and Elliott's proposal received widespread publicity. Apparently, however, the only official British act was an unaccepted recommendation to Mexico that she offer recognition in return for emancipation. Though admitting that abolition in Texas would be desirable, the British foreign secretary, Lord Aberdeen, assured both the Texas envoy and United States minister Edward Everett that Britain planned no interference with Texas. He had proposed a loan, said Lord Aberdeen, but his colleagues had refused to agree; the subject of slavery had not even been discussed in connection with the request.

In contrast, Calhoun's confidant and former editor, Duff Green, who was in England lobbying against the corn laws, reported that England had in fact offered a loan in exchange for emancipation. Calhoun and his friends chose to believe Green.

"If the Union Is to Break . . ."

So did the patriarch of Nashville, Andrew Jackson, who was still withstanding both his illnesses and the atrocious treatments of his doctors. Senator Robert J. Walker, who was involved in both land scrip and bonds, wrote Jackson a letter which drew upon the old man's hatred of all things British as a skilled violinist draws his bow. With equal skill Sam Houston assured his old commander that Texas had twice gone to the altar in a wedding dress. If abandoned a third time, the bride would seek another bridegroom. Houston had done enough courting to know the power of jealousy. Jackson responded with a long letter urging the immediate annexation of Texas.

Southern fears for Texas were paralleled by a growing northwestern appetite for all the Oregon Territory up to 54° 40', which was the southern boundary of Alaska. In 1818 the United States and Britain had agreed to a joint occupation, and in 1827 this had been renewed with a stipulation that either could end the agreement on a year's notice. By 1844 Americans had settled in the Columbia River area and had a reasonably clear title by right of occupation to the area now comprising Washington and Oregon. The British, meanwhile, had settled along the Fraser's river to the north. It was clear that Britain would not lightly surrender Canada's access to the Pacific, but for various northwesterners this was no argument. They would have "Fifty-four forty or fight!"

Anxious to get northwestern support for Texas, Robert J. Walker gave leaders from that section reason to hope that a grateful South would be happy to oppose Britain in the Far North as well as in Texas. Walker also made a remarkable emotional appeal to the Northwest in a public letter. Slavery, said Walker, was declining and would soon disappear in Missouri, Kentucky, and northern Virginia, and the states immediately northward might well be inundated by a mass migration

The Death of Slavery

of free Negroes. Texas, however, would open a gateway to the southward and provide an outlet for slaves and slavery to move not only into Mexico and Central America, but perhaps entirely off the North American continent. The letter shrewdly appealed to both racists and those anxious to spread America westward without the economic blight of slavery. Numerous Americans looking ahead to the future free states of Iowa, Kansas, Nebraska, Minnesota, and the Dakotas could take comfort from Walker's "safety valve" argument.

As Texas and Oregon came to dominate the press, the forgotten man in the White House, John Tyler, began to dream of annexing Texas himself and thereby winning reelection over his enemies in both parties. John C. Calhoun, meanwhile, again tasted the bitterness of disappointment as the narrowness of his Southern base of support daily became more apparent.

In 1843, Daniel Webster resigned as Secretary of State and was replaced by Calhoun's friend, Abel Upshur. Encouraged by the President, Upshur ignored the assurances of Minister Everett and assumed without question that the British were moving against slavery in Texas. Upshur offered Sam Houston a treaty of annexation and a promise of military protection against Mexico.

The path to statehood for Texas thus appeared to be wide open, but one stumbling block remained. The Texas constitution of 1836, in keeping with the later Texas reputation for thinking in big terms, had defined the boundaries of the new Lone Star Republic to include large parts of four other Mexican states, including almost two-thirds of present-day New Mexico. Since the Upshur treaty did not mention boundaries, Texans and Mexicans alike could only assume that the United States was preparing to support the Texas claims by force.

"If the Union Is to Break . . ."

Upshur's role suddenly came to a tragic end. On February 28, 1844, a happy bipartisan group of government leaders and their wives and friends boarded the USS *Princeton* for a Sunday cruise down the Potomac. A special attraction was the firing of a new rifled naval gun called the Peacemaker. In the morning the passengers marveled at the noise, smoke, and accurate trajectory. During a final exhibition enroute home in the afternoon, the Peacemaker exploded, killing six persons, including Upshur, Secretary of the Navy Gilmer, and David Gardiner. (Gardiner's beautiful twenty-three year old daughter had rejected an offer of marriage from the widower President. The tragedy changed the young lady's outlook, and President Tyler soon gained a bride.)

Because of Tyler's peculiar status with both parties, outstanding candidates for the vacant posts were scarce. Like Tyler, however, John C. Calhoun had also done some traveling between the parties, and he was available. Tyler reluctantly offered Calhoun the Department of State, and Calhoun "reluctantly" accepted.

The new Secretary promptly sent a military and naval force south to protect Texas, and on April 12, 1844, he signed the treaty begun by Upshur. Unless accompanied by conciliatory offers to Mexico, the treaty carried to its logical conclusion could mean only a war with Mexico or an abject surrender by Mexico of a vast area never part of the Mexican state of Texas. Land-hungry Americans both north and south, however, might still have supported the treaty but for Calhoun's next move.

Having signed a treaty which to be ratified would need all possible bipartisan and national support, Calhoun turned the question into a bitter sectional argument and an instrument for wrecking Van Buren's presidential nomination. After the *Globe* announced that Van Buren and his friends would whole-heartedly support the "reannexation" of Texas, Calhoun de-layed the announcement of the treaty for another week and executed a maneuver calculated among other things to change Van Buren's mind.

Just before his death Secretary Upshur had received an official letter from the British government emphatically deny-ing any plans against Texas slavery or against the interests of any other Southern state. The letter, however, ended on a moralistic note: "Although we shall not desist from those open and honest efforts which we have constantly made for pro-curing the abolition of slavery throughout the world, we shall neither openly nor secretly resort to any measures which can tend to disturb [the Southern states'] internal tranquillity."

To this brief statement Calhoun published a long answer which condemned the British for threatening slavery in Texas and the United States, announced his treaty of annexation, and concluded with a detailed eulogy of slavery as a wise and humane institution. Thus no Northerner could vote for the treaty without voting thereby for the moral righteousness of slavery. If Northerners would not do this, wrote Calhoun to a friend, it could only mean "that the spirit of faction and op-position to the South on the ground of slavery are stronger than the love of country."

Calhoun described his British correspondence as an oppor-tunity to force the slave issue which he intended to exploit to the fullest, and whether Texas itself or the opportunity for a showdown on slavery was his primary objective is impossible to determine. As early as December, 1843, the *Madisonian*, a Tyler-Calhoun paper in Washington, had stated that the defense of slavery required either secession or the incorporation of

"If the Union Is to Break . . ."

Texas, and this theme continued throughout the spring and summer of 1844. Representative Lewis of Alabama assured Calhoun that if the treaty were rejected he would "consider the Union at an end." Francis Pickens felt the South "bound in self respect and self preservation to join Texas with or without the Union." Governor Hammond of South Carolina added: "If the Union is to break there could not be a better pretext. With Texas the slave states would form a territory large enough for a *first rate power*. . . . The North and the South cannot exist united." Hammond insisted that "four-fifths of the South prefer Texas to the Union and are prepared to stand by that issue if made." In all these letters to Calhoun the writers clearly expected a sympathetic response.

On April 27, 1844, the leading contender of each party published a letter on the question of Texas. As expected, Henry Clay opposed immediate annexation. To the dismay of his ancient mentor, Andrew Jackson, Van Buren took a similar position. The Little Magician traced the history of Texas for six columns to show that Texas was legally part of the United States and should be and would be annexed, but he insisted further that the step should be preceded by termination of the war between Texas and Mexico and a settlement of the existing boundary disputes with Mexico. Two days later Jackson's other protégé, Benton, took the same ground and expressed the further heresy that the boundaries being claimed by Texas were unjustifiable. The *Globe* shocked Jackson further by praising Van Buren and Benton, although it stressed those parts of their letters which called for the peaceful and honorable annexation of Texas whenever this should become possible.

Old Hickory agonized over the Van Buren and Benton letters, concluded that Benton as the stronger must have been

The Death of Slavery

responsible, and found but slight comfort in a speculation that the *Princeton* explosion, which had knocked Benton unconscious, might have permanently damaged his old friend's brain. The old man fired a letter to the press reemphasizing his personal affection for Van Buren and explaining that the New Yorker had not been fully informed of the British threat and would surely change his position now that he understood the facts. It was an attempt to give Van Buren a second chance, but from New York came only silence.

Their all-out support for immediate annexation would have insured the Democratic nomination for Van Buren, kept Blair in his lucrative position as party editor, and left Benton's Missouri enemies impotent in a state hot for Texas. All three loved Andrew Jackson dearly and suffered from his displeasure. They were also professional politicians in the business of courting popular favor. For years, however, they had glorified their leader, Jackson, as an incorruptible and immovable hero who always did right regardless of the personal cost or danger, and they had been captured by the image they had created. Van Buren was obviously influenced by public opposition to the treaty in New York, and the other two men were affected by loyalty to Van Buren. All three, however, believed they were risking disaster entirely for principle, and their fury against Calhoun knew no bounds.

In the Senate Benton denounced the treaty as a threat of spoliation and robbery against Mexico, an attempt to promote disunion, and a bomb designed to blow up presidential hopefuls in favor of "a new Texas candidate, anointed with gunpowder." On June 8, 1844, the treaty was defeated by a 35-to-16 vote, with only eleven of the twenty voting Southerners supporting it.

"If the Union Is to Break . . ."

Calhoun described his mixed motives and double disappointment in a letter:

I had hoped to draw out a full correspondence by my letters to Mr. Packenham . . . and I Doubt not, what was intended would have been accomplished, had the Senate done its duty and ratified the treaty. Their neglect to do so, I fear, will not only lose Texas to the Union, but also defeat my aim in reference to the correspondence. . . . It will, I fear, be difficult to get another so favorable to bring out our cause so fully and favorably before the world. I shall omit none, which may afford a decent pretext for renewing the correspondence.

Benton's final apostasy came after he introduced a bill to annex Texas with certain conditions: a carefully defined boundary leaving the Rio Grande valley to Mexico; assent of Mexico to be obtained by treaty or omitted according to the will of Congress; and the creation of a single state of Texas as large as the largest existing state and the division of the remaining territory equally into slaveholding and non-slaveholding areas. This program, said Benton, would bring Texas into the Union without an unjust war with Mexico and without a sectional struggle which could cause a civil war. The bill lost by a small margin. In the debate Senator McDuffie of South Carolina warned that Calhoun's slain treaty, like Caesar's ghost at Phillipi, would haunt Benton in the forthcoming Missouri election. Perhaps so, answered Benton, but with one difference. Rather than take his own life as Brutus did, he would save himself "for another day, and for another use—for the day when the battle of the disunion of these States is to be fought—not with words, but with iron—and for the hearts of the traitors who appear in arms against their country." The words brought applause from the gallery and a handshake from an ancient enemy, John Quincy Adams. "Mr. Adams," said Benton, "you are passing off the stage, and I am passing away also, but while we live, we will stand by THE UNION."

News of a Benton-Adams handshake was almost more than Andrew Jackson could bear. "Do my dear Mr. Blair inform me if this can be true," the old man pleaded. "If it is, I want no better proof of his derangement."

Even before the treaty's defeat, the Democrats had met in convention at Baltimore on May 27. The telegraph was still a new toy, and anxious groups of people in Washington waited for reports on the newly strung wires between Washington and Baltimore. A combination of southern and western delegates engineered by Robert J. Walker established a two-thirds rule for the voting. Van Buren began with a considerable majority, but could not get the required two-thirds. The spirit of Andrew Jackson was present in favor of Texas immediately and all of Oregon, and ultimately the convention settled on Jackson's view that his fellow Tennesseean "Col. Poke" would be a good candidate. It was James K. Polk and a resolution that "our title to the whole of . . . Oregon is clear and unquestionable. . . . the reoccupation of Oregon and the reannexation of Texas, at the earliest practicable period, are great American measures, which this convention recommends to the cordial support of the democracy of the Union." Van Buren's New York friend, Senator Silas Wright, rejected the nomination for Vice-President, and the ex-President's only consolation prize was a resolution assuring him of "the deeply-seated confidence, affection, and respect of the American democracy." The convention closed on a high note. In his farewell speech, Chairman Wright of Pennsylvania was moved "to weep at the thought that this monument of mind before me must pass away, in the change of all things! . . . It will last, and be fresh on the pages of our country's history, when the pyramids of the Nile shall have crumbled, stone by stone, to atoms."

At the *Globe* Blair struggled to remain loyal to Van Buren and Benton, intercede for them with Jackson, and support the Polk candidacy. He and his partner John Rives also bet $22,000 on the election of Polk, a fact which pained his conscience every time he wrote an editorial against Clay's excessive gambling. Tyler's friends also nominated the President as an independent candidate. The *Globe* enjoyed attacking both Tyler and Clay until Tyler withdrew, and orders came from Jackson to support Polk and "let Tiler alone."

The election of 1844 was far from a popular mandate for Texas, and perhaps proved little more than Henry Clay's confirmed status as an unlucky politician. In New York the abolitionists, who were unsatisfied with Clay's view that at some future date under more favorable circumstances Texas might well enter the Union as a slave state, formed the Liberty party. Their candidate, James Birney, received almost 16,000 votes in New York, which Clay lost by only 5,000 votes. Had Clay won New York he would have been elected President by seven electoral votes. Nationally, the combined popular vote for Clay and Birney exceeded Polk's popular vote by some 24,000, but Polk had a substantial electoral margin.

When Congress met in December, 1844, the annexationists moved the simple admission of Texas to the Union by a majority action of each house. After a debate of almost three months, Walker won over the five Senate votes led by Benton by offering an amendment which gave the President a choice between the conciliatory Benton approach and the Calhoun program. Assuming that Polk would make the decision and assured by Jackson and others that Polk would stand on the Louisiana

The Death of Slavery

Purchase of 1803 in determining boundaries, the Benton forces capitulated. The joint resolution passed the Senate by a scant two votes. It also authorized Texas to divide itself into five states and extended the Missouri Compromise line on slavery. The first proposal, which would have given the South eight extra senators, was never seriously considered. The latter one was rendered meaningless by geography.

When the joint resolution was passed, the Tyler administration had three days left in office. Almost immediately an envoy was dispatched to Mexico with an unqualified and unconditional offer of annexation already approved by Congress. Boundaries were not mentioned.

The annexation of Texas had divided the Democratic party, opened the way to war and future territorial expansion, and irrevocably joined the process with a fierce sectional quarrel over slavery. It had become a manufactured political instrument as well as a national project, and in some ways an excuse for sectional discord as much as a reason. Whether or not any or all of this was necessary or inevitable was now purely academic. A train of events had been set in motion, and the end was nowhere in sight.

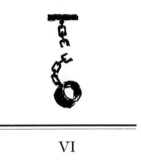

VI

For the Fulfillment of Our "Manifest Destiny"

Resolved: That the present war with Mexico . . . is now waged ingloriously,—by a powerful nation against a weak neighbor,—unnecessarily and without just cause, at immense cost of treasure and life, from which slavery has already been excluded, with the triple object of extending slavery, of strengthening the "Slave Power," and of obtaining the control of the Free States, under the Constitution of the United States.

LEGISLATURE OF MASSACHUSETTS

The annexation of Texas was entirely justifiable because that region had already won its independence. The additional territory taken from Mexico, however, was a different matter. The "manifest destiny" of the United States to become a continental nation and the weakness of the Mexican government's hold on

The Death of Slavery

the vast lands from New Mexico to the Pacific have satisfied the consciences of most modern Americans. It is true that Mexico ruled this area with frightful inefficiency and occasional oppression, and that the United States has since used it more wisely for the benefit of more people. The unique Mexican brand of slavery, Indian peonage, disappeared under American influence, the Mexican inhabitants kept their property and became citizens of the United States, and economic opportunities for the humbler members of society were probably increased by the transition. There is also reason to believe that California's substantial American minority, like the Texans, might have separated the area from Mexico without outside interference and thereby made it a natural candidate for peaceful annexation to the Union. Indeed, the peaceful surrender of New Mexico and the very minor resistance of California indicate a strong possibility that both might have been taken without a war if the United States had conceded the Mexican title to the territory between Texas and Mexico actually in dispute. Ironically, the war may have been caused in part by the feeling of American leaders that seizure of California would be dishonorable unless accompanied by a war for which the blame could be cast upon Mexico. None of this, however, alters the fact that the war began with a Mexican attack upon an American army which had advanced some 140 miles into territory that had never been in law or in fact anything but Mexican. In the end the only Mexican failing that counted was military weakness.

In 1819 the United States had relinquished all title to any of Texas in a treaty with Spain. The Mexican revolution had achieved independence from Spain for all of Mexico, including the Mexican province of Texas. The Texas boundaries established by Mexico could be changed by negotiation or by conquest, but not by a simple decree of the leaders of the new Texas. Had the Texans been able to take and hold any of the disputed territory by themselves, the United States claim would have been stronger, but the Texans could not claim the disputed areas by right of either conquest or occupation. Indeed, by 1843 the Texans had twice been repulsed in efforts to seize Santa Fe, New Mexico.

The Mexican War handed the United States a vast and fabulously rich area for a relatively small cost in blood and treasure. Ultimately, however, the price was compounded many times. Except for the existence of slavery itself, no single situation or event contributed so much to the coming of the Civil War as did the War with Mexico.

In 1845 the American presidency was not quite the isolated, Olympian pinnacle it has since become, and the responsibilities appeared less awesome in their magnitude. No President had yet been assassinated, although a young psychopath had contributed to the Jacksonian legend of invincibility by trying unsuccessfully to shoot President Jackson from a distance of less than a yard. The caps fired, but the charges failed to explode in his two pistols. The Presidents continued to go unguarded, and a presidential interview at the White House was a relatively easy matter for almost any ordinary citizen. Indeed, the harrassments of job-seekers were a major hazard of the office. For long periods of time no crises appeared, and the nation seemed capable of at least reasonable progress whether its leadership was strong, weak, wise, or atrocious. Numerous American Presidents left no personal mark on their nation at all. Occasionally, however, the character of the man in the White House was very important indeed.

"Who is James K. Polk?" sneered the Whigs in the cam-

paign of 1844. The election results answered the question partially, and Polk came to Washington determined to dispel any
lingering doubts as to his identity.

The mother of James Knox Polk was the great-grandniece
of John Knox, the founder of Scotch Presbyterianism, and her
son was equipped with a stubbornness, devotion to duty, and
independence worthy of this ancestor. Proud, sensitive to slights
both real and imagined, and always certain of the purity of his
own motives, Polk, like his mentor Jackson, rarely took a
tolerant view of his opponents. His wife, Sarah Childress Polk,
was beautiful, childless, and puritanical, and as first lady she
kept White House social life at a minimum. Their apparently
quiet and serene life together left Polk almost full time for
introspection and concentration upon his duty and his career.

After a highly successful period as a Tennessee lawyer and
planter, Polk served President Jackson well as a leader in the
House of Representatives. After fourteen years in the House
and a term of much power and influence as Speaker, Polk in
1839 surrendered a relatively secure seat to run for governor
of Tennessee. It was an unselfish attempt to save Tennessee
from what he considered the evil clutches of Whiggery, and
Polk succeeded, but for only one term. He was defeated for
reelection as governor in both 1841 and 1843, and he always
believed that his sacrifice and his efforts had gone unappreci-
ated. His plea for a new administration press in Tennessee had
gone unanswered, and he had felt neglected by the official
Democratic *Globe*.

By late 1843 Polk had his heart set on vindication by a vice-
presidential nomination, and he was resentful when the *Globe*
presented the claims of W. R. King of Alabama as well as his
own. The nomination for the top spot was a heady surprise,

For the Fulfillment of Our "Manifest Destiny"

but his victory was as much a challenge as a triumph. Too many Democrats regarded Polk as an accidental President of limited capacity, and hoped to make his administration a vehicle for their own ambitions. Aware of this almost to the point of obsession, the new President was prepared to take orders only from the Almighty and then only according to his own interpretation of the divine commandments.

Polk had many virtues and capacities, but the ability to reunite the Democratic party was not one of them. In the days of Jackson, Polk had fought side by side with Martin Van Buren, and his lingering respect and loyalty toward the leader he had supplanted was genuine. After exchanging several friendly letters with Van Buren, Polk offered the Treasury and War Department cabinet posts to the New Yorker's devoted friends Silas Wright and Benjamin F. Butler. Van Buren thought New York should have the State Department, but obviously this post could not go to anyone "soft" on Texas. Wright had already refused the nomination as Polk's vice-presidential running mate, and had since agreed to run for governor of New York. His rejection of the Treasury Department was polite but firm. Butler wrote Polk that he was willing to be Secretary of State or of the Treasury, but that the War Department would not be worth the personal sacrifices it would require. Two days later Butler received an unfortuitously delayed letter from Van Buren urging him to accept the War Department, and Van Buren's son, Smith, was speedily rushed off to Washington to assure Polk that Butler would reconsider, but it was too late. Polk was irritated by such temperamental irresolution, and various southerners and westerners had been working hard to convince him that the Van Burenites did not really matter anyhow. Smith Van Buren arrived to find that the War Department had gone to his father's New York enemy, William Marcy, and that Robert J. Walker was to be Secretary of the Treasury. The Van Burens immediately concluded that Polk had made insincere offers which he knew would be rejected, but most of the fault was clearly theirs. In a note to Martin Van Buren, Mrs. Butler took full blame for her husband's decision. The lady may have cast a long shadow. Had her husband become Secretary of War certain important events of the next four years might have come out quite differently.

Friends had already warned Blair that his *Globe* spoke too much for one faction of the party and had urged him to take a new partner more receptive to other viewpoints. Jackson's nephew, Andrew J. Donelson, was recommended, but Blair and Rives disliked Donelson for financial as well as political reasons. They had already lost money endorsing his notes. They would stand by their principles and take what came. Polk's personal feelings against Blair ran deep. He had been told the unlikely story that after his 1843 defeat in Tennessee Blair had said that Polk would be remembered by the Democratic party only when he redeemed his own state. Most important, the *Globe* was still loyal to Van Buren and Benton, and Polk, correctly enough, would share authority and prestige with no one. From the Hermitage Jackson urged the President to keep Blair and the *Globe*, but "Col. Poke" was his own man. He dismissed Blair as administration editor, and Blair, cooperatively enough, sold his paper to Thomas Ritchie of Richmond for $100,000. Blair could now develop his new Silver Spring plantation and build Jackson Hall (one story for rented stores and a restaurant, the upper floor for the Democratic party) with the $22,000 won on Polk's election. The dismissal was a personal humiliation, however, and caused much anger in Blair's wide circle of friends. Polk offered Blair the mission to

For the Fulfillment of Our "Manifest Destiny"

Spain, but the angry John Rives objected so strongly that he offered to pay Blair's ambassadorial salary if he would refuse. Rives' offer was not taken seriously, but his objections won out over the feeling of Blair's wife and daughter that a sojourn in Spain would be pleasant.

John C. Calhoun rejoiced in his enemies' apparent fall from influence, and hoped for a time that he might remain in the cabinet. On Jackson's advice, however, Polk offered Calhoun the mission to England, "there to combat with Lord Aberdeen the abolition question." Calhoun refused, and his friends were soon complaining that the local offices everywhere were going to "Benton, Blair, and the New York regency."

Worrying but little about the hurt feelings or disappointments of ambitious colleagues, the President outlined a herculean program and proceeded to work himself to death for its accomplishment. He would complete the Texas settlement for the maximum advantage of the United States. He would try to fulfill his campaign pledge on Oregon. He would take California because that Mexican province was unstable as Texas had been, and rumors had placed a British fleet in a threatening position. This Pacific prize, along with Oregon, was coveted by American commercial interests dreaming of a rich oriental trade, as well as by would-be settlers ready to start the covered wagons moving toward their final stopping place on the Pacific. A thoroughgoing Jacksonian agrarian, Polk would also push for a lower tariff and a renewal of Van Buren's independent treasury. James K. Polk was essentially a man of peace who loved the American Union and opposed anything and anyone who would sow discord among the sections. His most cherished goals, however, proved unattainable without war and the sharpest divisions within his party and the nation.

Few Presidents have ever asked or received less assistance

from a Secretary of State in reaching major decisions than did Polk. Secretary of State James Buchanan vacillated constantly, and the few strong positions he took were usually ignored by his chief.

With the annexation of Texas, Mexico had broken relations with the United States. Polk was willing to pay up to $40,000,-000 for New Mexico and California, but a channel of communications had to be reopened first. Unhappily, Polk's first unofficial envoy, William Parrott, held a much exaggerated financial claim against the Mexican government, and his arrival in Mexico City touched off a wave of popular anger which made the mere recognition of his presence impossible for any Mexican official or aspiring politician. Parrott was followed by John Slidell, whose status as "envoy extraordinary and minister plenipotentiary" made the United States itself the object of any insults he might receive. When the Mexican government flatly refused to discuss anything with Slidell except the Texas boundary, General Taylor was ordered to the mouth of the Rio Grande River. In part for recognizing Slidell at all, the Mexican government was overthrown on January 4, 1846, by a military regime pledged to resist every Yankee demand. In March Slidell gave up and returned home.

Slidell believed that the Mexican stubbornness was encouraged by a belief that the United States would have serious trouble with Britain over Oregon. Polk, however, was certain that if the United States lowered its tariffs on British manufactures and the British abolished their corn laws against American grains, the Oregon boundary would be no problem. Encouraged by the unanimous views of his cabinet, he pushed the Mexican quarrel to a showdown. Citing the insults to Slidell and the Mexican refusal to pay claims due American citizens,

For the Fulfillment of Our "Manifest Destiny"

Polk prepared a request for war. On Saturday, May 9, however, word came that General Taylor's army had been attacked north of the Rio Grande. The event occurred some 140 miles south of the border of the former Mexican state of Texas, but just north of the boundary set by the Texas Republic. On Sunday the President rewrote his request: Mexico had "shed American blood upon American soil." In his diary he also confessed a deep regret over having been compelled to work on Sunday. Within three days the Congress with but few dissents passed a declaration of war. John C. Calhoun blamed the entire business on Polk, and he and three followers refused to vote. Numerous others soon regretted their too easy capitulation to the excitement of the moment.

With one war underway, Polk also "looked John Bull in the eye" over Oregon. The President offered a compromise at the forty-ninth parallel. The British demanded the Columbia river valley. Polk advanced to a bold demand for 50°40′. The British receded to 49°. Reluctant to stand alone in violating his platform pledge for 54°40′, Polk asked the Senate for advice on the treaty before signing it. After a three-day speech by Thomas Hart Benton documenting fully the historical correctness of 49°, the exhausted Senate voted for its acceptance and on June 15 ratified the treaty by 41 to 14. The opposition was short on numbers, but long on noise. Northwesterners with sons and friends risking death in Mexico demanded "Fifty-four forty or fight!" but the only fighting was against Mexico for lands far to the South. Secretary Buchanan objected to Polk's sharp notes to the British on the ground that war might result, but later refused to draft Polk's message communicating the proposed treaty to Congress because it settled for less than 54°40′.

Northwesterners soon felt betrayed by the South again. With

the Senate margin only one vote, Congress passed the Walker tariff, which raised duties on luxuries and lowered those on necessities. Northwesterners helped the South pass the bill, but northwestern wool-growers felt sorely neglected. Also by a small margin Congress passed a new independent treasury system, and again northwesterners joined with an overwhelming Southern vote. Meanwhile, in a vote which appeared to be part of a bargaining process, Congress also passed a bill for extensive federal improvements on northwestern harbors, rivers, and lakes. The chief opposition came from the Southern friends of Calhoun. Receiving the rivers and harbors bill first, Polk kept it unsigned until delivery of the tariff and independent treasury bills. Then he vetoed the rivers and harbors bill on constitutional grounds. Some historians have called the bill a pork barrel measure, but northwesterners already angry over Oregon saw it differently. Chicagoans named the forbidding sandbar at the mouth of the Chicago river "Mount Polk," and charged the President and the slavocracy with indifference to their lives and property. Democratic and Whig papers alike took up the cry against the Slave Power, which was endangering the lives of sailors and stifling the progress of Northern cities, towns, and farms. After Texas was annexed, the Ohio abolitionist Joshua Giddings had announced that the "Union formed by our venerated predecessors" had been replaced by "a new slave-holding confederacy, with a foreign government." This was a gross exaggeration, but in 1847 it began to make sense to men who felt they had a God-given natural right to such blessings as protected markets, lighthouses, unencumbered harbors, snag-free rivers, and all of Oregon.

Northwestern bitterness against the South was more than matched by the fury of northeasterners who considered the war an unholy and wicked crusade in the cause of slavery. Indeed, the blood shed in Mexico was like oil thrown upon the fires of a sectional conflict hitherto only smoldering. *"Resolved,"* said the Massachusetts legislature by an overwwhelming vote:

That such a war of conquest, so hateful in its objects, so wanton, unjust, and unconstitutional in its origin and character, must be regarded as a war against freedom, against humanity, against justice, against the Union, against the Constitution, and against the *Free States;* and that a regard for the true interests, and the highest honor of the country, not less than the impulses of Christian duty, should arouse all good citizens to join in efforts to arrest this gigantic crime, by withholding supplies, or other voluntary contributions, for its further prosecution, by calling for the withdrawal of our army . . . aiding the country to retreat from the disgraceful position of aggression which it now occupies towards a weak, distracted neighbor and sister republic.

"If I were a Mexican," declaimed Thomas Corwin of Ohio on the Senate floor, "I would tell you, 'Have you not room in your own country to bury your dead men? If you come into mine, we will greet you with bloody hands and welcome you to hospitable graves.' " Praise for Senator Corwin rang throughout the North. As the war dragged on, Henry Clay and Daniel Webster, both of whom had opposed the policies which had produced the war, each received the somber word that a son had fallen. Public sympathy for the famous parents added further to the opposition to the war and the anger against the Slave Power.

Representative David Wilmot of Pennsylvania became the instrument of an inevitable Northern response with his proviso outlawing slavery in any new territories to be taken from Mexico. The proviso was an amendment to a bill providing money for negotiations with Mexico, and it became part of every appropriations debate for the next two years. In 1846 and 1847 it passed the House but was defeated in the Senate.

In February, 1847, Calhoun answered with a series of resolutions questioning the constitutionality of the Missouri Compromise and insisting that in all territories all states must have equal rights, including the protection of slavery. Otherwise, Calhoun grimly warned, "Political revolution, anarchy, civil war, and widespread disaster" would result. Benton charged Calhoun with "introducing needless firebrands to set the world on fire," while others from farther north were certain the Carolinian was plotting to steal the great Far West for slavery. Calhoun and his followers steadfastly opposed all appropriations for finishing the war and brought the slavery question into every debate. Regarding the slavery argument as dangerous foolishness for the mere sake of political ambition, the slave-holding President was soon denouncing Calhoun as "the most mischievous man in the senate to my administration."

As he grew thinner, paler, and ever more determined, Polk continued to suspect his fellow Democrats of putting 1848 ambitions ahead of 1846 and 1847 duties, and he struggled on with the war. The command of the armed forces is the one responsibility that most American Presidents have been least prepared for, and Polk was no exception. All in all, however, his correct judgments outweighed his mistakes, and he was in some respects uncommonly lucky.

Antonio Lopez de Santa Anna had successfully deceived the Spanish, the Mexican revolutionaries, the Church, and a long succession of both friends and enemies, and James K. Polk in 1846 was, therefore, the victim of both talent and experience. Soon after the war began, an envoy from the exiled Santa Anna in Cuba came to Polk with an offer to end the war on favorable terms for the United States in exchange for safe transportation back to Mexico. An American gunboat picked up Santa Anna, took him through the naval blockade, and landed him at Vera Cruz. With his usual sense of honor, the *caudillo* almost literally landed shouting denunciations of the United States, and he was soon appointed commander of the Mexican armies.

Santa Anna, however, was not a military genius, and his territory was infinitely vaster than his legions were numerous. Soon Thomas Hart Benton brought his old friend James Magoffin, a wily American trader from Santa Fe, for a long conference with President Polk. Magoffin returned to New Mexico, and when the American army under General Kearny arrived in New Mexico a few months later, the Mexican generals surrendered without a shot. The Mexican generals acquired unexplained affluence, and Congress later voted Magoffin $30,000 for undescribed services to his country.

Meanwhile, a joint effort from the sea under Commodore Stockton and overland by a small force under Captain John C. Frémont had easily conquered the vast and rich province of California. Unhappily for Frémont, General Kearny arrived soon afterward and assumed the governorship which Commodore Stockton had already conferred upon Frémont. Frémont was a remarkable blend of courage, energy, stubbornness, and stupidity. He was also the son-in-law of Senator Benton, and he had successfully defied superior authority once before when his eighteen-year-old bride destroyed some unwelcome orders and sent her supposedly unsuspecting husband off to explore the West with an expedition already ordered disbanded by the Secretary of War. Since he enjoyed being governor, Frémont chose to obey the navy, and when word from Washington finally vindicated Kearny, the Pathfinder found himself under arrest and facing court-martial on various counts of mutiny

87

and disobedience. None of this, however, interfered with the rapid and complete annexation of California by the United States.

These rich and easy conquests seemed to win the President but few friends outside the South, and the Whigs won both houses in the Congressional election of 1846. With most of Polk's objectives won, the problem of forcing Mexico to admit defeat and make peace remained.

The two leading major generals, Winfield Scott and Zachary Taylor, were reportedly Whigs, and Polk's personal relations with them became such that even intelligent communications were difficult. Polk's entire cabinet considered Taylor "unfit for command," and Scott had been something of a Democratic political problem since the days when President Jackson had relieved him of command during the ill-fated war with the Florida Seminoles. "Gen'l Taylor's feelings," Polk confided to his diary, "are anything but friendly to the executive Government. . . . He has no sympathies for the administration and cares only for himself." Taylor in fact did not favor territorial expansion and wished only for the war to end. The President considered Scott "not only hostile, but recklessly vindictive" toward himself and his administration. Scott was addicted to writing public letters, which the President usually considered treasonable at worst and "highly unjust and disrespectful" at best.

For many months Polk's chief military adviser was Thomas Hart Benton. The Missouri senator supported the administration's domestic programs and led the debates over military appropriations. He also presented Polk a military plan for an invasion at Vera Cruz and a march upon Mexico City, to be coordinated with a separate invasion from the north. In response to Polk's complaints about the disloyalty of his generals, Benton suggested the appointment of a chief with the rank of lieutenant general and with authority to plan overall strategy and negotiate for peace at the auspicious moment. The assignment, said Benton, would require statesmanship and wisdom as well as bravery, and if necessary he would take the job himself. The new rank, however, would require an act of Congress.

Various historians have derided Polk's attempt to create this post for Benton, but few contemporaries questioned Benton's competence. He had served as a colonel in the War of 1812, and as a longtime chairman of the Senate Committee on Military Affairs he knew both the personnel and the weapons of the armed forces. He was also well-versed in military history and strategy, had a thorough knowledge of Mexican geography, history, and politics, spoke fluent Spanish, and had numerous Mexican contacts. The plan failed because Whigs and Calhoun Democrats feared it would make Benton the next President, and because expansionist Democrats led by Walker, who wanted to annex all of Mexico, feared Benton would negotiate an excessively generous peace treaty.

Congress refused to create the new office, but after Polk had appointed Benton a major general, the House of Representatives voted to authorize the President to appoint his own commander-in-chief, regardless of seniority. By a small margin, the Senate refused to concur. Polk wanted Benton to go to Mexico as a major general, but Benton would go only as commander-in-chief with authority to make peace. The cabinet, led by Secretary of War Marcy, insisted that under existing law a junior major general could not be given command over his seniors. Polk was willing to recall both Scott and Taylor, but could think of no reason for recalling Generals Butler and

Patterson. Learning, however, that Butler was either ill or wounded in New Orleans, Polk urged Benton to wait for the possibility that General Patterson might also be eliminated. "I did not still see my way entirely clear to remove three senior Major-Generals who had rank of Gen'l Butler," the President wrote, "but thought it possible that I might do so in a short time." Benton, however, was not inclined to go to the front as the single replacement for four experienced major generals. It was the only sane decision, but the harrassed, overworked President considered it a shirking of duty. Relations between the President and the Senator were never again the same.

A few weeks later, Frémont arrived in Washington to stand trial for insubordination in California. Benton represented his son-in-law in a spectacular court-martial which ended in Frémont's conviction and dismissal from the army and, incidentally, made the young officer a national martyr. In review, Polk accepted Secretary Marcy's recommendation. He approved the findings, but remanded the sentence and ordered Frémont restored to full rank. Frémont and Benton, however, considered the trial a vendetta by West Pointers against an officer who had risen from the ranks. To them the approval of the findings was a mortal insult. Frémont resigned from the army, and his father-in-law never spoke to Polk again. Benton remained a loyal Democrat, but his alienation from Polk weakened the appeal of their party for many who still considered the Missourian the personification of Jacksonian Democracy. Frémont, who deserved most of his troubles, became a heroic symbol for Polk's enemies in both parties, and was destined to become the first presidential candidate of the new Republican party in 1856.

The war finally ended on a bizarre note. An earlier plan to

send a distinguished bipartisan peace commission was dropped because of opposition to Polk's insistence that John Slidell must be included. Secretary of State Buchanan did not want the peacemaking assignment, but he was also reluctant to give the opportunity to any future rivals in his own party. Neither he nor the President wished to send a possible presidential contender, even though it was their last chance to gain some credit for their party to offset the fame acquired by Generals Taylor and Scott. In the end, State Department clerk Nicholas Trist, husband of Thomas Jefferson's granddaughter and ex-secretary to Andrew Jackson, was dispatched to Mexico. As long as Trist quarreled with Scott over their overlapping authority, Polk considered his envoy incomparable. When, however, a gift of wine and jelly from Scott cured a stomach pain for Trist and a friendship developed, the President abruptly changed his mind. When Trist, like so many before him, was deceived by Santa Anna and granted a premature armistice which the wily Mexican immediately violated, Polk discharged Trist and ordered him home. Trist, however, in an action perhaps uniquely American, ignored his President's orders and eight weeks later signed a peace treaty. For $15,000,000 and the assumption of $3,250,000 worth of claims against Mexico the United States received New Mexico, Arizona, Utah, California, and Texas as defined by Texas. Polk was furious at Trist, but the unemployed civilian had driven a bargain no government could reject. The Senate ratified the treaty, but Trist received neither salary nor reimbursement for his expenses until 1871.

On February 21, 1848, while the Senate was debating Trist's handiwork, the eighty-year old John Quincy Adams collapsed at his desk in the House. Anxious friends carried him to the

The Death of Slavery

Speakers' office, where he lay struggling for life for more than forty-eight hours. A peaceful death finally came, however, and Old Man Eloquent lay stilled at last. Amid the eulogies by friends and foes alike, John C. Calhoun was conspicuously silent.

During the next twelve months President Polk watched his party ignore the ambitious cabinet members Walker and Buchanan and nominate a presidential candidate without asking his advice. Thanks in part to Secretary of War Marcy, who used the patronage of his office to strengthen the conservative New York Democrats, the liberal New York Democrats split off to form the Free Soil party. As a result, when the weary Polk left the White House for the last time in March, 1849, Zachary Taylor, the Whig general Polk disliked most, was waiting to move in. None of this made the retiring President very happy, but he returned to Tennessee firm in the conviction that he had served his nation well. Three months later he was dead. After many decades of neglect, history has concluded that his problems were indeed exceedingly difficult, his achievements impressive, and his failures not caused by any lack of devotion or dedicated effort for his country.

By the end of the Mexican War, the slavery question had a new dimension. Few Americans had thought seriously about tampering with slavery in states where it already existed. Its introduction into new areas, however, was a different matter. By keeping slavery out of the new territories, northeasterners could ease their consciences over a war considered wicked and unjust from the beginning, and in their region the awareness of slavery as a moral evil was most acute. Northwesterners, less worried about international morality and the inhumanity of slavery but

For the Fulfillment of Our "Manifest Destiny"

still smarting over Oregon, Polk's vetoes, and parts of the tariff, could fervently join a crusade to thwart the wicked and all-powerful slavocracy and keep the West a region of free land and free men.

To Southerners, meanwhile, the right to take slavery into new territories, even where geography and climate forbade it, took on a new symbolic value in the face of the Wilmot Proviso and the increased volume of the attacks upon their section. Calhoun's constant warnings had penetrated the surface of Southern feelings and stirred up their normal competitive instincts. People who feel they are sitting on a lighted bomb need reassurances, and perhaps the loud Southern demands for unusable rights in the territories were merely attempts to check the length of the fuse.

In 1848 Oregon received a territorial government with an antislave restriction, and the Whigs once again elected a general to be President of the United States. Oregon brought the slavery argument again to a blaze. The election created the Free Soil party and thereby became another important milestone on the road to civil war.

VII

Retreat from the Abyss

We . . . owe a great example to a struggling and
agonized world. . . . They see us almost in a state
of disorganization—legislation paralyzed—distant
territories left without government—insult violence outrage on the floors of Congress. . . . our an-
cestors . . . left us the admiration of the friends
of freedom throughout the world. And are we to
spoil this rich inheritance—mar this noble work—
discredit this great example—and throw the weight
of the republic against the friends of freedom
throughout the world?

THOMAS HART BENTON, 1849

There was peace with Mexico but a new conflict in Washington.
In far-off Oregon the settlers had outlawed slavery, and by
the spring of 1848 two Oregon delegates were begging Congress
for the blessings of a territorial government. Abolitionist John
Hale of New Hampshire introduced an amendment barring
slavery, and Calhoun replied that this meant "the degradation

94

of nearly one-half the States of this Union, who claim to be full equals here, and who intend never to yield that full equality." Come to Mississippi, said Senator Henry Foote to Hale, and we will hang you to our tallest tree. Be our guest in New Hampshire, replied Hale, and you will receive the respect due a senator. Hale withdrew his amendment, but the Southerners were equally adamant against the antislavery constitution proposed by the Oregonians.

Moderates pointed out that slavery was impossible in Oregon, and pleaded with both sides to stop the meaningless quarrel. "We read in Holy Writ," said Thomas Hart Benton:

that a certain people were cursed by the plague of frogs. . . . You could not look upon the table but there were frogs, you could not sit down at the banquet but there were frogs, you could not go to the bridal couch and lift the sheets but there were frogs! We can see nothing, touch nothing, have no measures proposed, without having this pestilence thrust before us.

The summer was long and hot, and tempers ran high. No one thought slavery could go to Oregon, and everyone agreed that with statehood Oregon could settle slavery in its own way. The principle of Southern rights in a territory, however, was debated as a life-and-death matter. In July a bipartisan committee proposed a compromise. Oregon should be organized with its antislave laws, and California and New Mexico should be organized with a provision against any action on slavery by their territorial legislatures. It was argued that any actual case involving slavery in California or New Mexico would be decided by the courts. If, as people expected, no slaves went there, the controversy would end. The Senate passed this compromise after an exhausting twenty-one hour debate. Before the weary members had recovered, however, the House had

The Death of Slavery

tabled their bill. After more weeks of bitter argument, the Senate in another all-night marathon voted to extend the Missouri Compromise line to the Pacific. Again the House disapproved. On the last day of the session the Senate debated until 9:00 A.M. Sunday morning amid fierce tensions and before crowded galleries. In the end, the two slaveholders Benton and Sam Houston joined with the North, and by the scant margin of their two votes, Oregon received a territorial government which barred slavery.

"The great strife between the North and the South is ended," said Calhoun. The bill would "convert all the Southern population into slaves. . . . The separation of the North and the South is completed. . . . This is not a question of territorial government, but a question involving the continuance of the Union."

The buckskin-clad Houston answered that slave restriction in a territory north of forty-two degrees could not possibly harm the South. He was "of the South, and he was ready to defend the South; but he was for the Union. The Union was his guiding star, and he would fix his eyes on that star to direct his course. . . . He would discourage every attempt to sow discord, and to stir up the passions of the country, and kindle them up to war."

The Oregon debates coincided with the early stages of the presidential campaign. The Democrats tried to neutralize the slavery issue and regain the Northwest by nominating Lewis Cass of Michigan. Cass had argued strongly that the people in each territory should decide the question of slavery for themselves. Cass had a record of achievement as a frontier leader and governor for eighteen years of the huge Michigan Territory (modern Michigan, Wisconsin, Iowa, and Minnesota). By 1848, however, he was sixty-six, fat, colorless, and uninspiring.

Retreat from the Abyss

Having won only one national election in their history, the Whigs sought to duplicate this feat by again nominating a candidate—Zachary Taylor—who could run as a military hero totally uncommitted on important issues. Jefferson Davis, whose first wife was General Taylor's daughter, momentarily encouraged the Democrats to consider Old Rough-and-Ready one of their own. Taylor, however, who had never voted, was persuaded otherwise by Thurlow Weed and William H. Seward, and perhaps by some of his quarrels with President Polk. The antislavery delegations from New England and Ohio opposed the slaveholding Taylor, but the Whig convention voted down a resolution affirming the power of Congress to control slavery in the territories, and in the end Taylor was nominated. Once again with a victory in sight, the great Whig statesman, Henry Clay, had been pushed aside by those for whom victory was more important than the principles or abilities of their candidate. No candidate of intelligence and proved ability—even one as moderate as Henry Clay—could fail to encounter opposition on the slavery question. The totally inexperienced and semiliterate military hero, on the other hand, had popular appeal, and could be marketed to the voters as a split personality on the slave issue. Taylor's campaign was managed by the antislavery New Yorker, William H. Seward, but it was vague enough to win the votes of most Southerners. Seward had no apparent difficulty reconciling his vaunted abolitionism with Taylor's ownership of more than a hundred slaves. It was all a sad commentary on the low state of American politics, and it was the beginning of the death rattle for the Whig party.

Almost equally important, when the Democrats convened, two delegations appeared from New York. In a typical Democratic effort at harmony, the convention voted to seat both and give each delegate half a vote, but the liberal Barnburner

The Death of Slavery

faction withdrew in anger. They soon met at Utica, New York, and nominated Martin Van Buren for President. Seven weeks later the Barnburners reconvened at Buffalo in company with other antislavery Democrats, Liberty party men, and "conscience" Whigs to form the Free Soil party. In a shouting, singing, roaring convention that resembled a religious revival, they renominated Van Buren with Charles Francis Adams as his running mate. Van Buren had engineered Jackson's first victory over Adams' father, John Quincy Adams, and had been a lifelong political enemy of the Adams family, but the union was entirely harmonious. Their slogan: "Free soil, free speech, free labor, and free men!" Their platform: "Opposition to the aggressions of the slave power," support for antislavery territorial governments, and demands for a tariff, a frugal government, river and harbor improvements, and free homesteads for actual settlers. The platform was appealing, and the party had quality—men like William Cullen Bryant, Francis P. Blair, Preston King, Samuel J. Tilden, Charles Sumner, C. C. Cambreling, and Salmon P. Chase. The major parties had the presses, the patronage, and the ties of past loyalty, however, and to most voters outside the Northeast the Free-Soilers appeared far more radical than they actually were. Van Buren and Adams received only 10 per cent of the total vote, but it was enough to defeat Lewis Cass. In New York, Van Buren outran Cass 120,510 to 114,318, and the New York electoral vote would have elected Cass. The Free Soil party fared remarkably well in the Northeast, and its leaders would comprise a Republican nucleus eight years later. Once again the Whigs had elected a President.

In 1850 the sectional quarrel reached a climax in a memorable session of Congress. The elder giants, Clay, Webster, Calhoun, and Benton, made their final Senate appearances and gave histrionic performances which have become monuments to their careers. Younger men like Seward and Jefferson Davis, however, spoke in new accents that would shape the future. The democratic process of debate, compromise, and acceptance of compromise was stretched almost, but not quite, to the breaking point. Compromises were finally possible in 1850 because there were concrete issues which provided the basis for give and take, and because in 1850 the extremists in Congress did not really speak for a majority of their constituents. The crisis developed naturally enough. In January, 1849, Calhoun renewed his attack with an "Address to the Southern Delegates in Congress," which warned that Northern opposition to slavery in the territories was only a step toward abolition and a bloody race war. The "Address" caused no great stir in Congress but received wide publicity in the Southern press. In October, 1849, Mississippi issued a call for the Southern states to meet in convention at Nashville on June 1, 1850, and the secessionists were clearly hoping that the impending quarrels would prove irreconcilable.

In January, 1848, the peace and serenity of Johann Sutter's great and beautiful California ranch were destroyed forever when an employee found gold near Sutter's Fort. Overnight some 100,000 immigrants scrambling for riches poured into California by land and sea, and every kind of lawlessness quickly followed. Amid the thievery, claim-jumping, violence, murder, and open vice, the desperate need for law and order was clear.

California had too many people and too many problems for territorial status. In September, 1849, a convention wrote a state constitution, and the people soon elected state officials and a delegation to Congress. A majority of the Californians were of Southern origin, and the first governor, lieutenant governor, and United States senators were Southerners, but the constitution forbade the introduction of slavery. When Congress met in December, 1849, California stood begging for admission to the Union. Since the United States was losing millions in gold from government land, and since California met every qualification for statehood, the admission should have been routine, but to various Southern leaders the antislave provision was a mortal insult. To Southern radicals, states' rights was a sacred principle for slaveholding states, but it was obviously not a blessing to be wasted on people who opposed slavery. One of the new California senators, incidentally, was John C. Frémont, who had returned to California to find gold and reach one of the high points of his up-and-down career.

Meanwhile, Texas was again in the limelight. The Texas constitution of 1836 had defined all of New Mexico east of the Rio Grande (two-thirds of the present state and the only part then with white inhabitants) as part of Texas. Twice during the brief period of the Lone Star Republic, Texans had invaded New Mexico. The first expedition of three hundred men had been imprisoned for several years, and a second force of two hundred men sent to intercept traders had been captured and disarmed by a United States military escort. The Texans considered their title a solemn obligation of the United States. When New Mexico surrendered to General Kearny, however, its people were promised that New Mexico would keep its traditional boundaries. The Federal government thus found itself with conflicting commitments.

Only the parties involved should have been concerned, but Texas was a slave state whereas New Mexico was a free territory. Slave state leaders quickly took the side of Texas, and practically everyone else felt sympathy for New Mexico.

Retreat from the Abyss

In March, 1848, Texas designated the disputed area Santa Fe County and appointed a judge for the district. Santa Fe papers recommended that the newly appointed judge bring soldiers to protect him from tar and feathers, and the stalemate continued. In September, 1849, New Mexico wrote a territorial constitution which ignored slavery, although slavery there had long been illegal, and the appointed congressional delegate stressed the impossibility of slavery in a well-publicized letter to Daniel Webster. In December, 1849, Texas subdivided the previous Santa Fe County into four smaller, equally theoretical counties and declared a showdown. The legislature called for mobilization, and public meetings all over the state demanded military action if necessary.

President Taylor, who had a fierce personal dislike for Texas, was determined to protect New Mexico. An agent was dispatched to New Mexico with promises of protection and instructions to the New Mexicans to stand firm and work for statehood. The appearance, at least, of a slow but steady collision course between a United States army and a Texas force supported by other Southern states was in the background of all congressional debates on the subject in 1850. On June 13, Henry S. Foote warned the Senate that one shot against Texas would bring every "heroic son of the South" and probably "hundreds of thousands of gallant and true-hearted men in the North" to the rescue. The result would be "Rivers of blood and scenes of butchery . . . more shocking than ever yet stained the pages of history." On July 3, President Taylor threatened to lead the United States army against Texas personally, and warned the unionist Whigs, Toombs and Stephens of Georgia, that if they rebelled he would hang them.

The long-standing demand for abolition in the District of

The Death of Slavery

Columbia, meanwhile, had been watered down to a far more popular movement for abolition of the slave trade in the District. The anomaly of the clanking chains, human pens, and shouting noises of slave auctions within earshot of the Capitol of a nation that claimed to be the freest on earth was obvious, but many Southerners still feared the action as a possible opening wedge to some future catastrophe. Less powerful, but also frightening to Southerners, was a budding movement against the entire domestic slave trade, and this proposal was especially obnoxious in states of the upper South which were steadily sending more and more of their slaves southward.

The major practical grievance of the South in 1850 was the loss of slaves who escaped to the North and could not be recovered because of the Underground Railroad, occasional help to the fugitives from individual northerners, a lack of police assistance in some states, and direct legal barriers in others. The actual number of escapees was greatly exaggerated, but this problem, like that of antislavery restrictions in far northern territories, had a symbolic significance. If Northerners were honest in their protestations that no attack on slavery in Southern states was intended, let them prove their goodwill by passing a federal statute to help Southerners regain their escaped property.

The Congress of 1850 began with a quarrel over the right of Father Matthew, a well-known Irish priest imported to preach temperance to New England working people, to be a guest on the Senate floor. Some twenty years earlier the good churchman had written an article criticizing slavery, and this was enough to deny him the privilege after two days of bitter argument. For seven weeks, sectional acrimony and useless quarreling prevailed, although there was time for a hot strictly

Retreat from the Abyss

party debate on a motion to sever relations with Austria because of the suppression of the Hungarian revolution. Ritchie's *Daily Union* dubbed the Whigs the Austrian Party, and roasted them for subservience to European tyranny.

Because of the Speaker's importance in selecting committees, the House remained without a parliamentary leader after sixty ballots and various threats of physical violence on the floor itself. The Free-Soilers held the balance of power and sought to make deals exchanging their support in the organizational process for assistance in their drive to bar slavery in the territories. Not until December 23 was Howell Cobb of Georgia chosen.

In January, 1850, the ailing Senator Henry Clay was almost seventy-three. Thirty years earlier Clay had authored the Missouri Compromise, and he was now prepared to leave the stage on an equally high note. Enlisting the support of Daniel Webster, who even in this final moment acted again in the shadow of Clay, the great Kentuckian offered his compromise: admit California with no congressional action on slavery, which meant a free California; give New Mexico and Utah territorial governments without mention of slavery; assume the Texas debt in return for Texas' relinquishing part of its claims against New Mexico; abolish the slave trade in the District of Columbia, but pass a resolution that slavery itself should remain there as long as it existed in Maryland or until Maryland and the District should accept compensation for a voluntary emancipation; give the South its fugitive slave law; and recognize the principle that Congress had no jurisdiction over the domestic slave trade.

Clay's resolutions provided a basis for concrete debate, and the halls of Congress soon rang with proffered amendments and roaring speeches. It was clear that very few were for all of the propositions, but that a majority for each was entirely probable. Four groups quickly developed: Northerners against any compromise; Southerners against any compromise; those professing support but insisting that all the propositions be passed in one bill; and those supporters who argued that each measure must be voted on separately.

On March 4, the dying Calhoun, wrapped to the chin in flannels, tottered to his Senate seat and informed a hushed crowd that a colleague would read his speech. Like Clay, the Carolinian remained in character to the end. The Southern states, said Calhoun, feared they could no longer remain in the Union with honor and safety, because soon there would be forty Northern senators against only twenty-four from the South. This in turn would mean the inevitable destruction of everything the South held dear. This inequality, insisted Calhoun, was due entirely to three types of government legislation: measures like the Northwest Ordinance of 1787, the Missouri Compromise, and the recent Oregon bill, all of which had denied Northern territory to Southerners; economic policies which had caused wealth to flow from South to North and thereby prevented immigration to the South; and, finally, those laws and precedents which had changed the federal republic into a consolidated democracy. No compromise, said Calhoun, could protect the South or save the Union. The North could save the Union only by conceding the South an equal right in the territories, enforcing the fugitive slave laws, ceasing all abolition agitation, and providing a constitutional amendment which would guarantee the South the power to protect itself. California was the test question, and the alternatives were plain. If the North would not agree to these requests, said Calhoun, "say so; and let the States we both represent agree to separate and part in peace. If you are unwilling we should part in peace, tell us so, and we shall know what to do, when you reduce the question to submission or resistance."

With all its tragic overtones and dramatic power, Calhoun's dying message was as inconsistent as the career it attempted to justify. Calhoun had spent years promoting the sectional discord he now deplored, and the threats and injustices he cited were grossly exaggerated. The Northeast and the Northwest were not united against the South on any question except that of extending slavery, and the South had more than held its own on most issues, including the recent acquisition of Texas. Common agrarian interests would keep the Northwest and South together on most economic questions, unless they should be divided by other factors. Calhoun declared that antislave restrictions barred all Southerners and implied that without the legal barriers the Old Northwest, Iowa, and Oregon would have become slave areas. Actually, many hundreds of thousands of Southerners had moved into the regions cited just to escape the slave system. Calhoun blamed the tariff for the lack of Southern immigration, but the duties had actually gone steadily downward since 1833. Slavery itself was the great deterrent against foreign and northern immigration to the South. Calhoun's charge that America had become a consolidated democracy in which the non-slaveholding states had a numerical superiority was correct. His corollary prediction that this would eventually compel the South either to secede or endure a forced abolition of slavery has achieved a certain faint validity in the ideological atmosphere and events of a century later, but it was not justified by the existing realities of 1850. In 1850 Congress had a long and consistent record of non-interference with Southern slavery. Constitutional abolition would have required an amendment which even in the later Union of fifty states the former slave states could block. There was no indication that the representatives of the most property-conscious people on earth would ever enact an unconstitutional law destroying Southern slave property and then vote the arms and men necessary to carry it out. Calhoun's final view that the South might secede in peace or successfully fight for independence would be tested later.

Three days after Calhoun's last speech, Daniel Webster rose for his final great oration. His role had been cast in the immortal "Reply to Hayne" in 1830, and he was still in character, but with a new tolerance and magnanimity toward the same foes. "I wish to speak today," said the godlike Daniel, "not as a Massachusetts man, nor as a Northern man, but as an American." The extremists on both sides, he said, were mistaken. Right could not be separated from wrong with mathematical precision, and the issues must be solved through mutual charity, concession, and compromise. In language almost arrogant in its self-confidence, Webster agreed with Calhoun that the American future lay with the free states, but he pleaded with his fellow Northerners to accept victory graciously and avoid insult to the South. The Wilmot Proviso, he said, was clearly unnecessary in California and New Mexico, and he would abandon it as a needless indignity to the South: "I would not take pains uselessly to affirm an ordinance of Nature, nor to reenact the will of God."

Having proffered the olive branch, Webster turned his guns full blast against the secessionists, including Calhoun, "who, I deeply regret, is prevented by serious illness from being in his seat today."

Retreat from the Abyss

"The Senator from South Carolina is in his seat," said a sepulchral voice.

Webster smiled and spoke directly to Calhoun: "Peaceable secession is an utter impossibility." Referring to the coming Southern convention at Nashville, Webster ridiculed the very thought of "hatching secession over Andrew Jackson's bones."

Webster sat down amid wild applause, but Calhoun was on his feet. "I cannot agree," he quavered, "that this Union cannot be dissolved. Am I to understand . . . that no degree of oppression, no outrage, no broken faith, can produce the destruction of this Union? . . . the Union *can* be broken." Webster answered that the Union could indeed be broken, but that such an event would be a revolution. Calhoun rose and tottered through the Senate door for the last time.

A few weeks later Calhoun died alone, leaving his last tortured effort on a few scraps of paper. The Constitution, he wrote, should be amended to provide two Presidents, one from each section, and no law should become effective unless signed by both. Calhoun's death brought a momentary pause in the general rancor, and his Washington funeral was magnificent. Clay, Webster, and other veterans rose to pronounce brilliant eulogies, but Benton was as silent as Calhoun had been after the death of Adams.

Webster, meanwhile, was denounced throughout New England for compromising with Satan. His constituents could accept the law of God against slavery in the territories, but his support for the fugitive slave law was another matter. "I know no deed in American history," said Theodore Parker to a great meeting in Boston, "done by a son of New England to which I can compare this but the act of Benedict Arnold." "Of all we

107

loved and honored," wrote John Greenleaf Whittier in the poem *Ichabod,*

> . . . naught
> Save power remains:
> A fallen angel's pride of thought,
> Still strong in chains.
>
> All else is gone; from those great eyes
> The soul has fled;
> When faith is lost, when honor dies,
> The man is dead!

Henry Clay, despite failing health, was never more eloquent in his appeals for reason and patriotism. Individual man, he said, was but "a mere speck upon the surface of the immense universe —not a second in time, compared to . . . eternity. . . . Let us look at our country and our cause; elevate ourselves to the dignity of pure and disinterested patriots, wise and enlightened states- men, and save our country from all impending dangers. What if, in the march of this nation to greatness and power, we should be buried beneath the wheels that propel it forward. What are we—what is any man worth who is not ready and willing to sacrifice himself for the benefit of his country when it is necessary?"

Calhoun was dead, but younger Southerners echoed his demands and looked to the future. To Jefferson Davis, Clay's program was no compromise at all because it gave the South nothing. Davis demanded the extension of the Missouri Com- promise line all the way to the Pacific Ocean, with the South to have full rights to take slaves to any territory, including California, south of the line. Even this would be a Southern concession, he said, and anything less would be an intolerable aggression. If the South, said Davis, "was to be debarred from acquiring by emigration, by enterprise, by adventure, by toil, and labor—equally with others, from the common domain of the Union," the Union would soon reach the condition predicted by Calhoun, "when, without an amendment of the constitution, the rights of the minority will be held at the mercy of the majority." Davis offered no specific amendment, but insisted that one was necessary to protect the South. Any denial of slave rights in the territories would "give additional power to a majority to commit further aggressions upon the minority," and to this he would never consent. Like Calhoun, Davis felt that all agitations against slavery must cease. Slavery, he said, required no apology. It had rescued the slave from barbarism and had given him civilization and the Bible. Indeed, he insisted, it would be good for California. Happily, the impossible demands of Davis for slavery where it had been rejected by a large population were not shared by most Southerners in 1850, but he would be heard from again.

Northerners like William H. Seward, John Hale, Salmon P. Chase, and others, opposed the Compromise as vehemently as had Davis. Seward, the sophisticated and inconsistent politician, spoke eloquently for this group when he denounced slavery as a sin against God's law, a "higher law" than the American Constitution. To the Seward of 1850 all legislative compromises were "radically wrong and essentially vicious," involving the "surrender of the exercise of judgment and conscience." Objecting to all compromise, Seward assailed this one in particular. It would, he said, exchange human freedom in other areas for "liberty, gold, and power on the Pacific coast." Seward struck boldly at the South's most sacred dogma. The Constitution, he said, did not really recognize property in slaves at all, because in both the three-fifths clause and the provision regarding the return of fugitives from labor, the Constitution used the word "persons." Indeed, argued Seward, slavery should not even be allowed to dominate the slave states, because in all of them freedom was a more important institution than slavery and the slaveholders were a disproportionate minority. Slavery was "only a temporary, accidental, partial, and incongruous" institution, while freedom was a "perpetual, organic, universal one, in harmony with the Constitution." And finally, avowed Seward, the founding fathers had permitted slavery only because it already existed. None of them would have voted to establish it anywhere. Indeed, no slave state with a choice would have founded slavery. Slave state leaders themselves had established freedom throughout the Northwest Territory. Britain, France, and Mexico had abolished it, and the rest of Europe was following suit: slavery was incompatible with all the world's best ideals and must not be established again anywhere.

Seward had struck the note which lacerated Southern feelings most—a moral disapproval backed by world opinion and based upon ideals shared by the South, and a refusal to grant Southerners even a shred of moral defense. Actually, Seward was entirely tolerant toward slavery where it existed, but Southerners found his bland assumption of moral superiority well-nigh unendurable. Obviously, Seward's point, which he himself did not really believe, that all legislative compromises were sinful could only mean rough days ahead.

Between the extremes of Calhoun and Seward were those who saw the necessity for compromise and welcomed Clay's high-minded idealism. Most of these, however, were determined to push for every advantage and save as much face as possible within the framework of Clay's proposals.

Most flexible was the proposition concerning New Mexico,

Retreat from the Abyss

and a substantial group of Southerners led by Henry Foote sought to control this question by combining all the measures in a single bill. By this they hoped to make a free California the price for amendments favorable to Texas and an insurance policy for the passage of the fugitive slave act. In the words of South Carolina's Andrew P. Butler:

The great object to be attained was this . . . there were three vessels at sea—one of them (California) was strong enough to carry the other and weaker vessels into port, if connected with her. California was a large and safe ship, and the other smaller boats in danger were to be attached to her, and she would carry them all safely into port.

In 1839 Foote had toured Texas and had written a two-volume history entitled *Texas and the Texans*. By 1850 he was second only to the Texans themselves in working for the annexation of New Mexico by Texas. Small, bald, and fiery, Foote had fought four duels and had been shot down in three of them. His exploits also included a rough-and-tumble fight with his Mississippi colleague, Jefferson Davis, and a wrestling match in the Senate aisle with the larger Senator Cameron of Pennsylvania. Offering the motion to admit the ladies to the gallery was part of his daily ritual, and he was always ready to provide them with a performance. Foote's overall influence was for the compromise, and his strategy for getting the maximum advantage for Texas was sound. His methods, however, contributed little to sectional peace.

Determined to save New Mexico, Thomas Hart Benton led those insisting that Clay's propositions must be dealt with singly. At first Clay himself agreed, and he and Benton, longtime enemies, were seen openly conferring. Foote, however, unmercifully taunted Clay for "forgetting the animosities of thirty years" and for treachery to the South. The sick and weary Clay

The Death of Slavery

saw that a combination was the best hope for Southern support, and finally agreed to support a move for a committee to write a single omnibus compromise bill.

For six long weeks the Senate argued over whether or not to form the committee. During these debates Foote attempted daily to provoke Benton into a physical attack. Over and over he taunted his older colleague with charges of falsehood, dishonor, and cowardice. Vice-President Fillmore refused to call Foote to order, and the normally hot-tempered Benton was remarkably patient. The inevitable day finally came, however, when the ponderous Benton rose and marched toward Foote. Foote drew a revolver and retreated down the aisle. "I have no pistols!" shouted Benton. "Let him fire! Stand out of the way! Let the assassin fire!" In the excitement a few Senators remained sensible enough to get between the antagonists. Benton was stopped, and Foote surrendered the pistol.

An investigating committee later absolved Foote of murderous intent, but charged that he had "without ... provocation, indulged in personalities ... of the most offensive character ... calculated to rouse the fiercest resentment in the human bosom." For most Northerners Foote's performance illustrated the violent nature of men corrupted by slavery. "ASSASSIN FOOTE," shouted the Northern press, and the event would be long remembered.

Foote later announced he would write a small book in which Benton would play a very prominent role. Benton answered that he would write a very big book in which Foote would play no role whatever. Each kept his word.

The omnibus committee was finally created, and after three weeks it produced a fair bill. For twelve more hot, bitter, weary weeks, the Congress debated amendment after amendment. Seward's group sought to add the Wilmot Proviso to the territories, while the Southerners tried one measure after another designed to give more of New Mexico to Texas. Fortunately, the Texas senators, Houston and Rusk, were Union men. They filled the air with pleas for justice, but they were entirely unwilling to create a dangerous showdown.

For some leaders political advantage was almost as important as reaching a settlement. Seward had a commanding influence with President Taylor, who wanted the immediate admission of a free California and the abandonment of the Texas claims against New Mexico. The presidential patronage was going to the Sewardites instead of to Vice-President Millard Fillmore, also of New York. Animosities toward Seward in both North and South became animosities also against the President, and Taylor responded with still greater efforts against the Compromise. This problem, however, was suddenly eliminated.

On July 4, the day after he had threatened to hang his Southern Whig friends and lead an army against Texas, President Taylor attended a celebration at the partly finished Washington Monument. He sat in the hot sun through an extremely long speech by Henry Foote, after which he slaked his thirst with great quantities of ice water and ate a few bowls of cherries with cold milk—which was probably germ-laden. After five days of suffering he was dead. The official diagnosis was typhoid fever.

The slaveholding Taylor had valiantly defended the Northern position, and he was a stronger President than his colleagues had expected, but his untimely death in 1850 probably helped America avoid civil war. The new President, Fillmore, hated Seward and was strong for the compromise. His favors would go to those accepting his version of patriotic reasonableness.

The Death of Slavery

After twenty-three more days of rancorous debate, the Senate suddenly passed amendments which split the omnibus bill into separate parts. The feeble Clay left for a needed seashore vacation, and Stephen A. Douglas of Illinois took command of the compromise. One at a time the measures passed much as Clay had proposed them. Texas abandoned its New Mexico claims, and the United States assumed $10,000,000 worth of Texas debts. The promised funds effectively smothered the Texas war talk.

The Southern disunion convention at Nashville, meanwhile, had been a failure. Most Americans both north and south wanted compromise and peace in 1850. Ordinary Southerners still could not easily identify antislave restrictions in far-off territories as a threat of Northern violence against slavery in the Southern states. Webster's talk of a future which belonged to the free states and his plea against the useless reenactment of divine laws had struck a responsive chord in the average Northern heart. Both sections were immensely prosperous, and the whole country was enjoying a new era of productive expansion. The riches of a vast continent were still beckoning to a people learning more and more new ways to use them. There were wildernesses to be conquered, farms to be created, towns and cities to be built, and forests, mines, and pastures to be exploited. Railroads and even newer modes of transportation would soon be needed. It was a land of matchless opportunity, and men everywhere rejoiced that the crippling disease of the slavery quarrel had been at least temporarily arrested. Compromise leaders, with the exception of Webster, returned home as heroes, and unionists in both North and South won most of the 1851 elections. Running on a Union platform, Foote defeated Jefferson Davis for the governorship of Mississippi.

Retreat from the Abyss

Even in South Carolina the unionists could still be heard, and those who would take action only in cooperation with other Southern states outnumbered those willing to go it alone.

The disease, however, was only arrested and not cured. The territory stretching from Texas to Canada and west of Missouri and Iowa remained unsettled. Slavery was apparently barred from the area by the laws of nature, but this did not eliminate the area as a further testing ground for Southern rights and Northern opposition to an alleged Slave Power. A fugitive slave act had been passed, but this did not mean that all Northerners would willingly surrender or help capture freedom-bound fugitives. The two-party system and the democratic process had been badly damaged. Personal hatreds and competitive animosities had received a further push. More elections and more clashes of ambitious politicians seeking votes and power lay ahead. New events would soon continue the process whereby the politicians' quarrel shared by only a minority in 1850 would become the peoples' war of 1861.

VIII

Some Ran Away

It is your privilege to catch your own slaves, if any
one catches them. . . . When you ask us to pay the
expenses of arresting your slaves, or to give the
President authority to appoint officers to do that
dirty work, give them power to compel our officers
to give chase to the panting bondman, you overstep
the bounds of the Constitution, and there we meet
you, and there we stand and there we shall remain.
We shall protest against such indignity; we shall
proclaim our abhorrence of such a law. Nor can
you seal or silence our voices.

JOSHUA GIDDINGS, 1852

On an October day in 1850, young William Craft and his
wife Ellen stood on the deck of a steamer and watched Boston
fade into the distance. They knew little of the England to
which they were bound, but their experiences since escaping
from a Georgia plantation two years earlier gave them reason
to expect kindness and generosity. They possessed enormous

116

Some Ran Away

courage, and the slender, thin-faced girl was gifted with histrionic abilities akin to genius. They had stolen clothes and money, and with the light-skinned Ellen masquerading as a young planter accompanied by William, her slave, they had made their way openly by train from Georgia to the North. The master and officials who had come to arrest them had met threats and intimidation from a vigilance committee headed by Theodore Parker and were still unaware of their flight by sea. If the Crafts felt nostalgia, it was known to them alone, but after the Civil War they would return voluntarily to Georgia.

In September, 1851, a Maryland slaveholder named Gorsuch was killed and his son was seriously wounded when they tried to recapture a slave at Christiana, Pennsylvania. The slave escaped. Several negroes and two whites were arrested for murder and treason. All were acquitted.

In June, 1854, fifty thousand hissing, groaning, and shouting people lined the streets of Boston as more than a thousand heavily armed soldiers, marines, and police escorted a trembling slave named Anthony Burns to a ship waiting to return him to Virginia. The cost of the capture was estimated at $100,000.

On January 27, 1856, Margaret Garner, her four children, her husband and husband's parents, and nine other friends walked across the frozen Ohio River to freedom. The friends escaped to Canada. The Garners were surrounded at the home of a kinsman. When all hope was lost, Margaret attacked her children with a knife, killing one and wounding the others. It was said that the dead little girl was very beautiful and almost white. The recovery of the Garners cost $21,456 in payments to four hundred marshals and became a major issue in Ohio politics.

On the night of December 20, 1858, John Brown led two

117

small raiding parties into Missouri. They directly and forcibly abducted twelve slaves from their masters' premises. One master was shot to death. The affair was widely publicized, and a $3,000 reward was offered for Brown's capture. Brown led the slaves almost twenty-five hundred miles through Kansas, Nebraska, Iowa, Illinois, Indiana and Michigan. On March 12, 1859, they crossed from Detroit into Canada. The efforts of William P. Clark of Iowa City and J. B. Grinnell of Grinnell, Iowa, had enabled them to ride a closed railway freight car from West Liberty, Iowa, to Chicago, but most of the journey was in the open. For this exploit Brown was never arrested.

There were other spectacular incidents, but not many. Few were needed, however, to convince Southerners everywhere that the North was filled with enemies blind to the Constitution and to all the laws of property. They were ultimately convinced that millions of dollars in slaves were being lost annually to Northern criminality.

Slavery as an institution was as remote to the average Northerner of 1850 as Russian Communism is to the average twentieth-century American, but an individual fugitive risking life and limb for freedom in 1850 was as real as an iron curtain refugee would be a century later. The very fact of running away appeared adequate proof of physical mistreatment, and where this was not true, the implication of an even greater spiritual torture aroused equal sympathy. Fugitives who had lived in obscure safety in Northern towns for several years prior to 1850 suddenly found themselves endangered—and just as suddenly found themselves with many new friends determined to defy the South's new law.

The 1850 law was uniquely designed to inflame Northern consciences. Marshals or deputies could be fined $1,000 for noncooperation with a pursuing master, and any person helping a fugitive could be fined $1,000, imprisoned six months, and assessed $1,000 in civil damages for each slave escaping through his efforts. For obvious reasons the fugitives were provided no jury trial, and a claimant's affidavit was usually sufficient evidence of title. Hearings were conducted by federal commissioners, who received $10 if the fugitive was awarded to the master, but only $5 in case of a release. There is no evidence that any commissioner ever enslaved a free man for the extra $5, but the legalized temptation only made sharper the Northern view of the tyrannical and corrupting power of the Southern slavocracy.

The new law quickly brought to a peak of organization the Underground Railroad system whereby Northerners in almost every state organized their efforts to help the fugitives. Circulating information among slaves and sending former fugitives back to the South as leaders, organizers, and guides; hiding fugitives in secret rooms, basements, churches, barns, caves, and thickets; and transporting them by night and day through all manner of ingenious ruses, more than three thousand Northerners at one time or another helped slaves make their way from Southern plantations and homes to Canada.

Assuredly, the significance of even one human being seeking freedom cannot be taken lightly, but the extent of the fear, bitterness, and hatred between the sections generated by the fugitive slave problem rested in part upon a gross exaggeration of the numbers involved. The United States census indicates that the annual loss was less than 1 per 5,000 slaves. In 1859, 803 slaves escaped, and 500 of these were from border states. The border states, which suffered most of the losses, showed little excitement. The Deep South, from which escape was almost impossible and which lost a mere handful—only 16 of the 400,000 slaves in South Carolina escaped in 1850—was in constant fury over the allegedly massive Northern depredations. Similarly, in the border states of the North to which all slaves had to escape at first and in which most of the recaptures occurred, protest was at a minimum. In far-off New England, Michigan, and Wisconsin, where slave-catchers were almost never seen, the press, politicians, and pulpit kept up a constant din against Southern kidnapers. At least one historian of the Underground Railway has judged from the boasting of ex-Railroad workers and the depth of Southern anguish that the census figures reveal only a fraction of the actual losses. The figures were provided by Southerners, however, and it is unlikely that people who were publicly broadcasting their grievances at every opportunity would have minimized them when dealing with the census-takers.

The fugitive slave issue apparently developed no great zeal on the part of most Northerners to attack the South with physical force. It did, however, increase Northern determination against humoring the South with concessions, however meaningless, in the remaining territories, and it helped prepare Northerners to believe the worst of any charges made against the South.

The cost of regaining a slave was frequently greater than his value, and the commercial value of the known runaway was immediately depreciated. Every Northern act of assistance to a runaway, however, was by implication a moral condemnation of the institution and the South itself. This, rather than the actual economic losses, probably caused the greatest Southern fear and anger. The question contributed much to the ultimate Southern secession. The creation of a separate Southern nation would only move the freedom line from Canada down to the

Some Ran Away

Ohio River, but the illogicality of this solution struck few secessionists in 1860.

It is remarkable that such a dramatic and emotional theme as the struggles of people to escape slavery produced only one major work of literature, but it is natural that the book which gained a virtual monopoly of the subject should have enjoyed such an enormous popularity.

If Harriet Beecher Stowe had no authentic experience with Southern masters, plantations, or slaves, she had considerable contact with fugitives. *Uncle Tom's Cabin* was her first literary venture, but she was gifted with the ability to breathe life into her characters from the moment they spoke. The aspirations, fears, sufferings, frustrations, nobility, and villainies of her characters can still be felt intensely by every reader. The book quickly became an all-time best seller, and as far away as Russia masters liberated their serfs after reading it. It showed slavery at its worst, and put countless readers into the shoes and skins of the slaves themselves. Southerners pointed out in vain that in real life situations and events such as hers rarely if ever happened, because it was clear that everything in the book was entirely possible. Despite Mrs. Stowe's conscious effort to avoid condemning Southerners as such, the Yankee-born overseer, Simon Legree, became a cruel stereotype of the Southern slaveholder. Similarly, the saintly Uncle Tom, the heroic George Harris and Eliza, and the delightful Topsy became the typical slaves in the minds and emotions of Northern readers.

Critics have argued that Mrs. Stowe exaggerated the virtues and capacities of the average slave at this particular stage of his cultural development, and a few still attribute this alleged backwardness to innate racial inferiority. Others, with far more logic and evidence, blame it upon the crippling effects of slavery itself. Some have suggested that the unfortunately premature investment of the still uneducated and inexperienced Negro with great political power in the South during Reconstruction was due in large part to the excessively optimistic view of his superior nature as taught by *Uncle Tom's Cabin*. Another recent author, however, insists that Mrs. Stowe with all her good intentions was essentially a racist who helped create unfavorable stereotypes of Negro character that still plague his quest for legal and social equality. This argument cites her paternalistic attitude, but draws most of its evidence from the later plays and "Tom" shows that were only remotely based upon her original story. Among the slaves' descendants, at least, Uncle Tom has come half circle from his original status as a slave hero to a symbol of cowardly acquiescence to white indignities.

Whatever the later judgments, the book was a major spur to sectional conflict. It strengthened the righteous resolve of Northerners to help fugitives and to insist upon legal barriers against slavery in the territories, however unsuited for slavery they might be. Its enormous popularity contributed much to the growing Southern paranoia. Being out of step with the civilized world on a great moral question is deeply painful, and many Southerners, if only subconsciously, must have recognized the conflict between the noble ideals supporting their own right to freedom and their convictions about slavery. Fanatical zeal is often the product of profound doubt and insecurity.

IX

Bleeding Kansas and Bleeding Sumner

> They never shave or comb their hair, and their chief occupation is loafing around whiskey shops, squirting tobacco juice and whittling with a dull jack knife. They drink whiskey for a living, and sleep on dry goods boxes—are all "national democrats," and delight in robbing hen roosts.... Their conversation is interspersed with original oaths, and generally ends in a free fight. They are "down" on schools, churches, and printing offices, and revel in ignorance and filth. After visiting them one cannot but feel the truth of the doctrine of total depravity.
>
> "CHICAGO TRIBUNE" DESCRIPTION OF PROSLAVE MISSOURIANS IN KANSAS

On a balmy afternoon in June, 1852, Mr. and Mrs. Franklin Pierce were enjoying a leisurely carriage ride through the pleasant New England countryside near Boston when a friend galloped up with exciting news. After the better-known leaders like Douglas, Cass, Buchanan, Marcy, and Butler had been exhausted by the struggles against each other, the Democratic national convention on the forty-eighth ballot had nominated Franklin Pierce for President of the United States. Mrs. Pierce listened intently to the messenger and then fainted dead away.

Several months later, President-elect and Mrs. Pierce and their only child, an eleven-year-old son, were still savoring their triumph as they rode along on a train from Boston to Concord. Suddenly the car lurched and tumbled down an embankment. Young Benjamin Pierce died before his horrified parents' eyes. His mother never fully regained her sanity, and social life at the White House during the Pierce regime was almost non-existent.

The problems of a grieving, suffering wife did not make President Pierce's job easier, and he was at best ill-equipped for its responsibilities. His rivals for the nomination had fallen one by one because each had well-known convictions and the enemies that went with them. Pierce had neither deep convictions nor enemies, but he would soon correct the latter deficiency. John Letcher wrote Pierce that he confidently expected protection for the South. On the same day, David Wilmot wrote the new President his expectation that Pierce would check the South.

For a candidate the Whigs had again turned to a military hero, General Winfield Scott. Henry Clay was dying, attended in his illness by Mrs. Francis P. Blair. The Blairs had loved Clay in their youth, but had later fought him bitterly for twenty-five years. In his final days, the old Kentuckian achieved mutual forgiveness and reconciliation with the Blairs, Van Buren, and Thomas Hart Benton in turn, as the old enmities faded into insignificance beside the new perils facing the American Union. Daniel Webster had hoped for a final chance, but he too was nearing death, with the voices of countless erstwhile admirers still calling curses down upon his vote for the fugitive slave bill. Nominated by a party split in half by the fugitive slave act, Scott was overwhelmed by Pierce at the polls, and the Whigs had no national leader to replace Clay and Webster. Northern and Southern Whigs would henceforth go their separate ways, each in search of a new allegiance. The Whig party died with Scott's vanishing hopes, and its efforts for national unity would be sorely missed.

If the Compromise of 1850 was to endure, its defenders would need all possible help from the White House. Unionists North and South had won most of the 1851–52 elections, and Pierce might well have been expected to strengthen their hands with his major appointments. Radicals and moderates of both sections begged for cabinet posts and equated the President's kindly words with commitments. In the end, however, Pierce ignored the unionist friends of Douglas in the Northwest and the recently victorious Southern moderates. Instead, he bowed to Southern extremists with two appointments totally lacking in political wisdom. Jefferson Davis, recently defeated by a conservative unionist for governor of Mississippi, became Secretary of War. Caleb Cushing, highly talented, but despised in his native Massachusetts because of pro-Southern sympathies, became Attorney General. The two soon came to dominate their leader. In diplomatic appointments also, Pierce gave the plums to extremist Southerners and their friends. Union men everywhere, and especially in the South, felt deserted by the Democratic party and its new administration.

The Southern influence in foreign affairs was quickly felt. In late 1853 Pierce in the Gadsden Treaty gave Santa Anna $10,-000,000 for a narrow strip of desert south of Arizona and New

The Death of Slavery

Mexico. The land was considered worthless, and the only obvious reason for the purchase was to gain a right-of-way for a new railroad from California to New Orleans or Memphis. The treaty roused angry Northern opposition.

In October, 1854, the longtime Southern dream of a new slave state in Cuba flowered in the famous Ostend manifesto. American ministers Buchanan from England, Mason from France, and Soulé from Spain, met in Belgium to issue a public offer to buy Cuba coupled with an open threat to take it by force if necessary. Spanish anger was exceeded only by that of American Northerners, and the project was hastily disavowed by the administration.

Meanwhile, in January, 1854, Northern anger at the South had agained reached a new height.

Stephen A. Douglas, the Little Giant from Illinois, was five feet four, almost as wide as high, and a tough, ruthless political battler. He intended to be President some day, and though only forty he was not one for extended waiting. He knew what the slave issue had done to the Whig party, and he hoped to save his own Democrats from a similar fate. His political future as well as his hopes for a growing, united America required a slavery formula upon which Northern and Southern Democrats could agree.

Douglas was also a land speculator with enormous faith in the future of his home city of Chicago. Obviously the eastern end of the California railroad should be in Chicago. The senator was also chairman of the Committee on Territories. It was his duty to get territories organized, and lying in the path of his proposed railroad route to California was the vast area to become Kansas and Nebraska. A railroad through these virgin regions would require liquidation of Indian titles, new territorial governments, and occupation by the usual horde of frontiersmen waiting for new lands. A bill for these purposes almost passed in March, 1853, and by December the situation had become pressing. Southerners wanted a southern railroad route, and Secretary of War Jefferson Davis already had the army engineers surveying their way toward the new Gadsden purchase. Closer home, former Senator and now Representative Thomas Hart Benton was beating the drums for a route to St. Louis, and the pictures of trade and intercourse with the Orient painted by his soaring imagination and thunderous oratory had roused people all over Missouri. Indeed, Benton had already been to the Kansas border to make speeches urging Missourians to force the territorial issue by moving into Kansas ahead of any legal action.

Drafting a bill for organizing Kansas-Nebraska was routine, but certain Southern leaders threatened opposition because the territory would be automatically free under the provisions of the Missouri Compromise of 1820. Particularly noisy was Senator David Atchison of Missouri. President of the Senate and crude and forceful, Atchison was under pressure from Missouri slaveholders anxious to avoid another neighboring haven for fugitive slaves, and he could not accept a Kansas bill for which the hated Benton might claim some of the credit. The bill must provide a concession to Missouri slaveholders and if possible be unacceptable to Benton. Atchison easily persuaded other Southern senators, although the real depth of their opposition to a bill which would not mention slavery is difficult to measure. Some observers, including the not unprejudiced Benton and one Abraham Lincoln, later insisted the matter had not disturbed the Southern people and that the measure could have passed without disturbing the sacred compromise. Certainly,

127

The Death of Slavery

continued obedience to a thirty-three year old law originally passed with heavy Southern support could not be regarded as a new insult to the South. Douglas, however, wanted a broad Democratic consensus as well as a majority vote for his bill. He was convinced that slavery could never go to either Kansas or Nebraska, and believing most people to be equally realistic, he concerned himself only with finding a face-saving solution for all concerned.

The doctrine of popular sovereignty, or simply allowing the territorial settlers to decide the matter of slavery for themselves, had occasioned no great criticism when first enunciated by Lewis Cass in 1848 and later incorporated in limited form in the Compromise of 1850. To Douglas it was the obvious panacea. The Missouri Compromise, he hoped at first, could be left unmentioned unless Southerners actually took slaves to Kansas, and this he was certain would not happen.

The inconsistency between popular sovereignty and a federal statute barring slavery, however, would not down. After days of private arguments, Whig Senator Dixon of Kentucky on January 15, 1854, offered an amendment repealing the Missouri Compromise, and Douglas reluctantly accepted it. President Pierce, weak and indecisive, listened to Jefferson Davis as well as to Douglas and the Southern Senators. The administration would support the repeal.

The realistic Douglas had not realized that others were less realistic than himself. To the Northern public the repeal of the Missouri Compromise looked too much like a Southern conspiracy to steal the great West for slavery. A group headed by Salmon P. Chase, Charles Sumner, Benjamin Wade, and Gerrit Smith immediately published "An Appeal of the Independent Democrats in Congress to the People of the United States," which swept rapidly across the country in the press and pulpit. The "Appeal" was based upon the false premise that a prospective belt of midwestern slave states from Texas to Canada was about to rob all free men of their western birthright, but it found readers ready to believe the worst. The "Appeal" denounced this "gross violation of a sacred pledge; as a criminal betrayal of precious rights; as part and parcel of an atrocious plot to exclude from a vast unoccupied region, immigrants from the Old World and free laborers from our own States, and convert it into a dreary region of despotism, inhabited by masters and slaves."

In some of the fiercest parliamentary scenes in American history, Douglas fought back with the theme that all informed men knew that geography and climate barred slavery from the region.

At least two elderly statesmen agreed with Douglas but saw his mistake in its larger implications. The old Texas hero, Sam Houston, six feet six and tough as ever, stopped whittling and rose to spurn this alleged favor to his section. This useless measure, he said, would only convulse the country from Maine to the Rio Grande, and he would have no part of it. "If this repeal takes place," he warned, "I will have seen the commencement of the agitation, but the youngest child now born, will not live to witness its termination."

In the House, Houston's old commander and friend, Thomas Hart Benton, was even more explicit. Half the Union would be arrayed against the other in deadly hostility, he warned, and by an action suggested "not by the inhabitants—not by anyone living, or expecting to live in the territory . . . but by a motion in Congress—a silent, secret, limping, halting, creeping, squinting, impish motion, conceived in the dark—midwifed in a committee room, and sprung upon Congress and the country in the style in which Guy Fawkes intended to blow up the parliament house."

The two old comrades knew their America well. People, large and small, who cared little for the sufferings of the slave or the sins of his master, reacted violently against the possibility of a blighting slave desert blocking the access of free men to the Pacific. To northwesterners especially, the traitorous repeal of the Missouri Compromise was just another in a long line of wicked interferences by evil slavocrats in the glorious destiny of America which could be realized only when men like themselves had occupied the continent. And a further insult was added when the vociferous opposition of Germans and other immigrant groups led to an amendment denying aliens the right to vote or hold office in the new territory. Attacks on the bill by Northern newspapers, politicians, and preachers soon swelled into a new chorus of invective against the South itself, and their Southern counterparts, after a surprisingly long period of puzzled apathy, ultimately responded in kind.

After four months of name-calling and fierce debate, numerous supporters, including the President, wished they had never heard of Kansas, but Douglas kept them in line and the bill passed.

Immediately, Eli Thayer launched what became the New England Emigrant Aid Society to send deserving antislavery land-seekers to Kansas. Popular sovereignty would get an assist from the righteous. Dozens of similar companies appeared in various states, but Thayer's organization remained the prototype. At first, success came hard because Kansas, after all, was fifteen hundred miles away. In 1854–55 only 1,240 signed up, and Garrison complained that there was hardly an abolitionist among them. Then Kansas held its first territorial elections.

Bleeding Kansas and Bleeding Sumner

The Kansas-Missouri border had long been crowded with mule skinners, trail guides, trappers, Indian scouts, buffalo hunters, speculators, gun salesmen, and the usual run of lawless drifters and adventurers attracted to every frontier. It would perhaps be no coincidence that the only United States President produced by western Missouri would be noted for aggressive toughness. Such men had long considered Kansas their own, and excited in part by Benton's loud insistence that Indian titles were already clear enough to permit a settlement, they had almost reached the limits of patience before Douglas introduced his bill. Indeed, they had already crossed the border by the hundreds to stake out their future claims. Almost none of them owned any slaves, but they were mostly from the slave state of Missouri, and what was good enough for Old Mizzou was good enough for them. The continuation of the Missouri Compromise would not have affected their ambitions in the least, but its repeal made slavery legal if they wanted it. Missourians would demand every right coming to them whether they expected to use it or not. When word arrived that New England Yankees had organized a multimillion-dollar corporation to send abolitionists out to grab off the choice lands of Kansas, the cause of slavery suddenly assumed a symbolic value totally unrelated to economics. Frontier editors and politicians had no trouble whatever in rousing most of western Missouri into a state of armed alert.

Despite the noise, however, no serious problems developed beyond the usual barroom murders and conflicts over land claims, town sites, and county seats, until November, 1854, and March, 1855, when first a territorial delegate to Congress and then a territorial legislature had to be elected. By the end of 1854, the small number of slaves in Kansas, the widespread racist objections to the presence of any Negroes, whether slave

The Death of Slavery

or free, and the obvious reluctance of slaveholding emigrants to risk Kansas when Arkansas and Texas also beckoned, had already indicated clearly that Kansas was destined to become a free state. Missourians, however, had their pride. In both elections a wild throng of Missourians, some of them half-drunk, crossed the border to vote. More than seventeen hundred Missourians voted in November, and a proslave delegate went to Congress. In March more than five thousand Missourians repeated the performance of November. Former Senator Atchison—the Bentonians had beaten him in the 1854 election—led eighty armed voters personally, and assured them there would be enough Missouri voters to "kill every God-damned abolitionist in the Territory."

Stealing an election, however, could not make Kansas a slave state. Indeed, the effect was the opposite. The almost defunct emigrant aid societies revived rapidly as word of these "slave power" outrages swept across the North. More and more Northerners poured into the region, but the actual patterns of conflict and violence differed but little from those on other frontiers. In fact, with somewhat less whisky and little talk of slavery, Iowans were sharing with equal enthusiasm in the early affairs of Nebraska. Kansas, however, was a battleground between nominal proslavers and crusaders for freedom, even though the crusaders themselves wrote a constitution which forbade forever the entry of any Negro—free or slave—into Kansas. Abolitionists who filled the United States Congress with passionate oratory in support of this constitution conveniently ignored this "black law" provision.

Kansas was quickly blessed with numerous newspaper correspondents ready to fight against slavery and squeeze the last drop of blood from "bleeding Kansas" for the benefit of their eastern readers. In the Northern press, every victim of violence, whether the affair involved a card game, romantic competition, claim-jumping, or just general orneriness, was a martyr for freedom at the hands of a mob of tobacco-chewing, whiskey-sodden, oath-breathing, depraved Southerners. The Southern press tried to respond in kind, but like their emigrant aid movement, such efforts never achieved much conviction. An essentially normal frontier struggle thus became bleeding Kansas, the first battle of the Civil War.

"I believed," wrote the abolitionist correspondent James Redpath, "that a civil war between the North and South would ultimate in [slave] insurrection, and that the Kansas troubles would probably create a military conflict. . . . Hence I . . . went to Kansas; and endeavored, personally and by my pen, to precipitate a revolution." In Redpath's reporting the cold-blooded murder and horrible mutilation by cutlasses of five alleged proslavers in one night by John Brown became a proslave outrage.

"I have no choice," said Brown to wavering followers. "It has been ordained by the Almighty God, ordained from eternity, that I should make an example of these men." For Redpath this explanation was entirely adequate. The famous "sack of Lawrence" caused only two casualties, both proslavers and both accidental victims of the excitement and free-flowing whiskey. In the Northern press the event became a major holocaust featuring, according to Redpath, pyramids of fire, the booming of cannon, two rapes, and two hundred stolen horses.

William A. Phillips of the *New York Tribune* went to Kansas "not only to write well, but also . . . to fight well." His book of what were essentially fairy tales, entitled *The Conquest of Kansas, by Missouri and Her Allies*, became a free state bible, and later made him a Kansas senator. Another reporter found reading his *Chicago Tribune* in the midst of the proslavers like reading the Scriptures in secret during the reign of Bloody Mary.

As the victims of Southern bestiality, including at least one young woman ravished and left for dead while returning from "one of the outbuildings in the rear of the house," continually multiplied in the Northern press, harsh criticisms of all things Southern increased proportionately. Bleeding Kansas was now ready to furnish the lifeblood for a new northern political party.

> With regret I come again upon the Senator from South Carolina, who . . . overflows with rage at the simple suggestion that Kansas has applied for admission as a free state, and with incoherent phrases, discharges the loose expectoration of his speech, now upon her representatives, and then upon her people. There was no extravagance of the ancient, parliamentary debate which he did not respect, nor was there any possible deviation from truth which he did not make, with so much of passion, I gladly add, as to save him from the suspicion of intentional aberration.
>
> Were the whole history of South Carolina blotted out of existence, from its very beginning down to the day of the last election of the senator . . . civilization might lose—I do not say how little; but surely less than it has already gained by the example of Kansas against oppression. Ah, Sir, I tell the senator that Kansas, welcomed as a free state, will be a ministering angel to the Republic when South Carolina, in the cloak of darkness which she hugs, lies howling.

The tall (six feet four), handsome speaker was Charles Sumner, Senator from Massachusetts, and the words were part of an eight-hour oration which generated great heat but shed little light upon the actual problems of Kansas. Senator Andrew Pickens Butler, the object of Sumner's special attention, was an elderly gentleman who, like most Southerners, frequently spoke strongly on sectional questions. He did not use abusive language, however, and off the floor he was popular with colleagues from both sections.

Sumner was a genuine idealist of great ability. He was also overbearing, egotistical, and self-righteous. His only marriage ended in failure after a few months—reportedly his bride could not stand living with God. Once, when told that Sumner did not believe in the Bible, Ulysses S. Grant, in a rare flash of wit, answered, "That's because he didn't write it." To Charles Francis Adams, Sumner was "a tremendous egotist and woefully lacking in common sense."

The attack upon Butler served no useful purpose. Freedom of speech and immunity from libel prosecution on the floors of Congress are necessary for a free, effective parliamentary government, but they presuppose a certain mature restraint on the part of the lawmakers. Even the most heinous accusation, if documented, can be offered in a reasonable and unemotional manner. "That damned fool will get himself killed by some other damned fool," said Stephen A. Douglas, himself ridiculed as "the Sancho Panza of slavery" in the speech.

The defense of family honor was and is more obligatory in Southern society than elsewhere in America, and Senator Butler had a young and vigorous nephew in the House of Representatives. After two days of brooding and sleepless nights, Representative Preston Brooks of South Carolina marched to the Senate floor and shattered his cane against the head of Senator Sumner.

The Senator was painfully hurt, but did not lose consciousness. Estimates of the number of blows ranged from six according to Southerners up to three dozen counted by observant Northerners. All agreed that the hollow, gutta-percha cane was destroyed beyond repair. Dr. Boyle reported two scalp wounds of approximately two inches each. One healed immediately but the other became infected. This was corroborated by Doctors Miller and Linsley, who reported much improvement in the infected wound after they had opened and drained it. At this point, Sumner's brother and Dr. Perry from Boston took charge of the case. The ailing Senator was taken to the Silver Spring plantation of Francis Preston Blair, where, presumably, he was cared for by Blair's slaves, and alarming bulletins about his condition began appearing regularly.

The earlier doctors' description of Sumner's swollen lymph glands indicates that he probably did suffer an extreme crisis from infection, but it is equally likely that a rapid cure ensued once the initial infection was overcome. Sumner, however, did not return to the Senate for three and a half years. During this long period he toured Europe seeking medical assistance. His travels were spiced by a social life of furious energy, and included a traversing of the Alps on muleback because he felt too weak to walk. "I have been in the Pyrenees, in the Alps, and in the Channel Isles," he wrote a friend. "You will next hear of me in the Highlands of Scotland." A Parisian doctor diagnosed the ailment as a sprained spine which caused deep pain with each deep thought or emotion. Modern students of psychosomatic illness would have understood Sumner's problems.

The extent of Sumner's injury, however, is of academic interest. More important, a personal brawl due to an insult to an aged relative quickly became another national struggle between slavery and freedom. Massachusetts offered to pay all medical bills, to which Sumner replied, "Let whatever Massachusetts can give go to suffering Kansas." Yale and Amherst granted the Harvard-educated statesman honorary degrees.

"The surgeons of the City of Washington," was the toast of

136

Bleeding Kansas and Bleeding Sumner

Oliver Wendell Holmes at a medical society dinner. "God grant them wisdom for they are dressing the wounds of a mighty empire and of countless generations." The *New York Tribune* echoed the spirit of hundreds of public meetings attended by throngs of angry and excited Northerners: "A thorough-going and consistent advocate of slavery would not scruple at a lie or false oath or hesitate at murder." Beecher, Evarts, Wayland, Emerson, Everett, and Bryant brought excited crowds to the point of hysteria with their descriptions of the attempted assassination. To the British minister, Cornwell Lewis, it was "the first blow in a civil war." Bleeding Sumner had joined bleeding Kansas.

In the South, Brooks was widely criticized for making the Senate floor an arena, but it was generally agreed that Sumner deserved the caning. After the Northern press had vilified Brooks as an assassin and described his act as typical of the slaveholding morality, the South rallied to his defense. New canes, at least one inscribed "Hit him again," were sent to Brooks, and editorials and resolutions praising his "act of justice" appeared all over the South.

The Northerners had their own heroic bully boy in Senator Benjamin Franklin Wade, a tough frontier type from Ohio. Wade insulted Southerners and the South in language even more direct than that of Sumner. When challenged to a duel, Bluff Ben chose squirrel rifles at twenty paces with each man to pin a white piece of paper over his heart. The challenging Southerner denounced Wade as a barbarian and no gentleman, and the duel was never fought. For the rest of the decade, Wade roamed the Congress like a modern Goliath, taunting his colleagues and daring any and all comers to physical combat—and, strangely enough, finding no Southern David willing to accept

The Death of Slavery

his terms. In 1858, Wade, Simon Cameron of Pennsylvania, and Zachariah Chandler of Michigan announced a compact whereby they would make the personal quarrels of any offended Northern colleague their own. For some Southerners the prospect of a new Southern senate without Wade in it may have been a subconscious force working for secession.

By 1856, the personal antagonisms in Washington itself, the demise of the Whig party and the need of commerce and industry for a party, the rage of Northern Democrats who felt betrayed by the Kansas affair, the lingering resentments of Free-Soil elements left from 1848, and the longtime hope of the abolitionists for influence in a major party had combined to produce a new Republican party. The party began with various fusion movements in several Northern states in 1854, and by 1856 it was ready for a national convention. Francis Preston Blair, slaveholder, Free-Soiler, and former editor and aide to Andrew Jackson, served as chairman, and the delegates in the convention hall included men who had been his enemies for a quarter of a century. Democrats like Blair, Preston King, Salmon P. Chase, and William Cullen Bryant were now ready for common cause with Whigs like Seward, Thurlow Weed, Thad Stevens, and Horace Greeley.

The Blairs were powerful in the new party, and the 1856 candidate was their choice. John C. Frémont had played an exaggerated but well-published role in opening the Oregon trail and conquering California, and he had been a martyr in the hated administration of James K. Polk. The fact that he had deserved his court-martial was irrelevant. The dashing "Pathfinder," born and bred in South Carolina, was an outspoken enemy of slavery and slave-expansion, and his father-in-law was the still popular ex-Senator Benton. A Whiggish economic

138

program headed by the slogan "Free Soil and Free Men" was the Frémont platform.

The Democrats convened in Cincinnati, with Douglas eager for the nomination but still young enough to wait. There was a free-for-all fist fight between two competing Missouri delegations, but Northern and Southern Democrats ultimately found harmony in the nomination of James Buchanan. By spending four years as minister to England, the Pennsylvanian had avoided the battles which had weakened the other aspirants. The two bitter enemies, Douglas and Benton, each saw hope in Buchanan.

A third party was in the field in 1856. There was brutal competition for jobs in the burgeoning new Northern mills and factories, and efforts to gain better wages and working conditions were weakened by the seemingly inexhaustible supply of cheap immigrant labor. Unions were as yet almost non-existent, and an attempt to turn the law of supply and demand to the benefit of labor by restricting immigration appeared to be a logical solution. Also, of course, many of the newcomers were Roman Catholics. Authors and publishers willing to promote hatred and suspicion at a profit were not lacking, and the vicious nonsense in their books and pamphlets provided a moral justification for cruelties dictated primarily by self-interest. In the mid-1850's, various American cities suffered bloody riots in which helpless immigrants were murdered in cold blood by nativist mobs. By 1856 this combination of fear and bigotry had produced the American or Know-Nothing party, which drew most of its organizational strength from the former Whigs. The Democratic rank and file were also seriously affected, although the Democratic party remained firmly on record against such tactics and was clearly identified in many areas as the party of the immigrant. A substantial number of immigrants, especially the Germans, were also strongly attracted by the Republican platform against slavery extension.

Meeting in convention, the Know-Nothings nominated former President Millard Fillmore, who had never been a member of their party and who could not even be consulted because of his absence in Europe. Fillmore, personally the antithesis of fanaticism, persuaded himself that the party could become a new political home for conservative Whigs unwilling to join the Republicans and a new rallying point for national unity. Presumably, Northerners and Southerners were to submerge their slavery conflict in a common front against a greater danger —the prospect of America's inundation and destruction by a horde of Catholic workers dedicated to betraying America into the hands of the Pope. The platform accepted popular sovereignty as a solution to the slavery quarrel.

In 1856, therefore, America's presidential choices were a dashing hero lacking in common sense but running on a platform in step with democracy's highest ideals; a former President campaigning from the best of motives but representing a party dedicated to the worst of human emotions; and a professional politician hitherto noted only for indecisiveness and subservience to Southern interests.

Frémont was not even on the ballot in the South, and the fire-eaters spread the alarm far and wide. The election of a Free-Soil President, they argued, would leave the South no honorable alternative but secession. Calmer Southerners pleaded that their section had as yet suffered no real indignities and that even if Frémont were elected, he should be given every opportunity to prove that he meant the South no harm. Whether the ordinary Southerner believed the frightening predictions of so many of his leaders cannot be determined. He continued with his business and voted for Buchanan.

In keeping with the spirit of the times, both Democrats and Know-Nothings charged that Frémont was a Catholic. In 1841, Frémont had bowed to the will of his seventeen-year-old fiancée, Jessie Benton, and consented to an elopement. After several Protestant ministers, probably fearful of the wrath of the bride's father, Senator Benton, had refused to perform the ceremony, the young lovers had found a brave Catholic priest. The record of this Catholic ceremony was adequate proof for Frémont's opponents, and Frémont, who moreover had much strength among immigrant voters, did not dignify the charge with a denial.

Frémont's father-in-law, Benton, was still popular, and his expected support had been an argument for Frémont's nomination. Old Bullion, however, sadly parted company with his favorite daughter and son-in-law. In a forty-day period, the old man delivered twenty speeches calling for the election of Buchanan—whom he personally detested. America, he said, must not elect a purely sectional President, or a civil war would follow.

Fierce animosities are a by-product of the competition of every American national election, and 1856 produced even more than its share. The war in Kansas shared headlines with the presidential candidates, and for Republicans Frémont was the Galahad who alone could save the territory and the West in general from slavery. Frémont attracted to his banner some of the purest idealism ever generated in 'American politics, but in the end too many Americans recognized the dangers which would follow his election. The national candidate, James Buchanan, was elected, but Frémont ran a powerful second with

The Death of Slavery

114 electoral votes to the victor's 174. Buchanan carried only five of the sixteen free states, and Frémont had a popular edge of more than 100,000 votes over Buchanan in the free states. Southerners were left painfully aware that without the Know-Nothings Frémont might have been elected, and that a few shifts here and there might easily elect a Republican in 1860.

X

The Political Quest for
Peace and Votes

I would give them any legislation for the reclaim-
ing of their fugitives, which should not . . . be more
likely to carry a free man into slavery, than our
ordinary criminal laws are to hang an innocent
one. . . . If we could arrest the spread, and place
it where . . . it *would be* in the course of ultimate
extinction, and the public mind *would* . . . believe
that it was in the course of ultimate extinction, the
crisis would be past and the institution might be
left alone for a hundred years, if it should live so
long, in the States where it exists.

ABRAHAM LINCOLN

James Buchanan was not a particularly happy man. Many years
before, his fiancée had died suddenly under mysterious circumstances while the young Buchanan was on an extended
business trip to another city, and her parents had forbidden him

to attend the funeral. His neglect was allegedly related to the tragedy, and for this real or imagined cruelty the young man had vowed to atone by remaining faithful to her memory for the rest of his life. As a Washington bachelor he gravitated naturally to the gay, convivial Southerners who most often left their own wives at home. For many years fellow bachelor William R. King of Alabama was his best friend. Lacking any deep convictions on political issues, and apparently with no moral antipathy toward slavery, Buchanan all too often allowed his personal affections for individual Southerners to determine his political actions.

The new President's road was made no easier by the final message of the retiring Franklin Pierce. Bitter over his own rejection, Pierce lashed out at the Republicans as radical fanatics bent upon destroying America with a bloody race war. The congressional session preceding Buchanan's inauguration was spent largely in rancorous debates over the justice or injustice of Pierce's accusations. When Buchanan appointed Southerners to most of the important cabinet posts, the anger left by Pierce boiled again to the surface.

James Buchanan, hater of controversy, grasped for straws of peace in his inaugural address. Popular sovereignty, he said, was a fair solution to the territorial problem, and the Supreme Court would soon rule on the question of just when the settlers could make their fateful decision on slavery. Almost petulantly he begged Americans to accept the decision of the Court, turn away from conflict, and get on with the more important business of developing America.

If Buchanan had any previous knowledge of the expected Court opinion, his address showed an abysmal ignorance of the Northern public mind. The Dred Scott decision ignored both

The Political Quest for Peace and Votes

Northern sentiment and all precedents related to the principle it sought to establish. It was also perhaps the most unnecessary opinion ever rendered by an American court.

Ostensibly the freedom of slave Dred Scott was at stake. In reality all parties concerned had long since agreed that he was to go free as soon as his usefulness as a liberty-seeker should be ended. Scott had lived in the free state of Illinois and the free territory of Wisconsin as the slave of army surgeon John Emerson. After returning voluntarily with his wife and children to St. Louis with the doctor, Scott found himself in difficult straits after his master died and the widow could no longer support a slave and his family. After supporting the Scotts for some time, the son of a former owner finally financed Dred in a suit for freedom on the grounds that residence in the free areas had made him free. The first trial went against Scott. The second ended in his favor. By this time the territorial quarrel gave the case a new meaning. Mrs. Emerson went to Massachusetts and married an abolitionist. Rather than simply grant Scott his freedom, she transferred him by a fictitious sale to a brother, who went through the motions of resisting Scott's pleas until the case reached the Supreme Court of the United States.

The Court, headed by the venerable Roger B. Taney, a former radical Jacksonian Democrat, at first decided that the status of a slave in Scott's circumstances should be decided by the courts of the slave state. This opinion was supported by numerous earlier precedents, but Justices McLean and Curtis submitted long dissents covering the entire question of territorial slavery. In response to McLean and Curtis, Taney and the majority, none of them slaveholders, produced a long discourse covering the same ground, although the actual verdict remained unchanged.

The Death of Slavery

Taney argued in effect that no Negro could be a citizen, and that Scott, therefore, could not sue in a federal court. Since citizenship was still a matter of state jurisdiction, this judgment was entirely unwarranted. Then Taney lit a fuse. The Congress had been ruling territories as it saw fit since the Northwest Ordinance of 1787, and this power had always been accepted by the courts, the Congress, and the people alike. Taney, however, ruled that the Constitution followed the flag—that the citizens of any American territory, regardless of its qualifications for statehood, had the same constitutional rights, obligations, and powers as the citizens of the existing states. Slaves, he reasoned further, were recognized as property in the Constitution, the Constitution decreed that no citizen could be deprived of property without due process of law, and the Congress, therefore, could not bar slavery in any territory. The already dead Missouri Compromise had been unconstitutional from the beginning.

The Dred Scott decision did not put a single slave in a single western territory, and later courts reversed its basic principle in dealing with overseas territories. It returned Scott to slavery, but he was immediately set free and in fact finished his life as a railroad porter. For many Americans in 1857, however, the ruling seemed just another step in the onward rush of the slave power to spread the wicked institution across the continent. Republicans still smarting from the denunciations of Pierce and angry over Buchanan's pro-Southern leanings remembered the President's inaugural address, and charged a conspiracy among Buchanan, Taney, and Douglas. The next decision, warned countless newspapers and speechmakers, would impose slavery upon the states themselves.

The Political Quest for Peace and Votes

Taney's decision coincided unhappily with the final efforts of the Kansas proslavers. Because the Kansas Free-Soilers, who were in the majority, refused to vote either for delegates to a new constitutional convention or on the question of slavery after the constitution was finished, the proslave party was able to present Congress with the ratified proslave LeCompton constitution and ask for statehood under its terms. And for once, James Buchanan made a firm decision. To restore sectional harmony he demanded the immediate admission of Kansas under this constitution.

These combined efforts of Taney, Buchanan, and the Le-Compton Democrats would have ruined a lesser man than Stephen A. Douglas, who was compelled by both expediency and principle to support Taney but to fight Buchanan and the LeCompton constitution. Douglas faced an election campaign in 1858, and the people of Illinois would make no concession to the South beyond popular sovereignty and would tolerate popular sovereignty only so long as it spelled freedom. Beyond 1858, however, lay 1860, and Southerners would never support a presidential candidate who dared repudiate the Dred Scott decision. Reconciling a court decree which denied the right of territorial citizens to prohibit slavery with a doctrine advocating the right of settlers to decide the matter for themselves required considerable imagination, but Douglas had it. The Court's view that any citizen could take slaves to any territory was correct, he announced, but the right would be useless unless local territorial legislatures passed the necessary police regulations for its enforcement. Thus popular sovereignty was still the practical solution.

More pressing, however, was the LeCompton constitution.

147

The Death of Slavery

"By God, Sir," said Douglas, "I made James Buchanan, and by God, Sir, I will unmake him." With no apparent hesitation, Douglas joined his Republican enemies in the battle against the admission of Kansas with the proslave constitution. The usually placid Buchanan was roused to anger and ordered all loyal Democrats to combine against Douglas. Illinois newspapers supporting Douglas were deprived of government advertising and printing, and local officeholders were ordered to organize public meetings against him.

Other Northern Democrats had also supported popular sovereignty in the faith that it would mean a free Kansas and were fully aware of the danger to themselves if it did not. After many weeks of fierce debate, the Douglas Democrats and Republicans passed a bill which gave Kansas another election, and in August, 1857, the Kansas Territory officially rejected slavery forever.

American politics had a strange new alignment. The Republicans had won Kansas for freedom, but they had lost it as a political issue. Their party needed a new program and new leadership. Stephen A. Douglas had led the fight against the LeCompton constitution and was in the eyes of President Buchanan no longer a Democrat. Perhaps the Little Giant and his sweeping ambitions for the economic development of an expanded America could be recruited for the Republican party. At least Horace Greeley and several other Republican leaders hoped so. Illinois Republicans who had spent years fighting Douglas, however, disagreed.

A house divided against itself cannot stand. I believe this government cannot endure permanently half slave and half free. I do not expect the Union to be dissolved; I do not expect the house to fall; but I do expect it will cease to be divided. It will become all one thing, or all the other. Either the opponents of slavery will arrest the further spread of it, and place it where the public mind shall rest in the belief that it is in the course of ultimate extinction, or its advocates will push it forward till it shall become alike lawful in all the States, old as well as new, North as well as South.

The speaker was Abraham Lincoln, and his oration was designed to convince Republicans and Free-Soilers everywhere that Stephen A. Douglas had no place in their ranks. Only a few hours before, an Illinois Republican convention had rebuked Horace Greeley and other national leaders for their new feeling toward Douglas by declaring Lincoln the party's official candidate for senator against Douglas. In response, Lincoln argued with occasionally specious facts and logic, but with magnificent political acumen, that slavery, if unchecked by law, would take over the free states. Douglas, he continued, had no moral objections to slavery, and the house divided could become all free only by entrusting the government to leaders who considered slavery morally wrong and would put it on the road to ultimate extinction.

The "house divided" image was politically risky and later cost Lincoln some needed votes, but "ultimate extinction" was a product of sheer political genius. It could mean tomorrow or a thousand years hence, depending upon the hearer or reader.

This is not to say that Lincoln was consciously cynical in his choice of words. He had often expressed a moral revulsion against slavery, but as a child of the upland South, and, indeed, of his times, he considered the Negro race inferior, and was painfully aware of the problems which would accompany the disappearance of the institution. He had no discernible ambition to tamper with Southern slavery at the risk of further sectional conflict, but up until the Kansas-Nebraska act he had apparently found comfort in a faith that at some point in the distant

The Death of Slavery

future some new set of circumstances would permit its peaceful destruction. By his own public testimony, at least, it was the moral indifference implied in popular sovereignty rather than its practical results that had roused Lincoln's ire. All hope for the eventual death of slavery required a continued moral repugnance toward slavery by the public, and the institution's permanent confinement within its present limits. Thus, according to Lincoln, every possibility of slavery expansion, however remote in fact, must be opposed for symbolic as well as practical reasons. Since the anti-Negro sentiments of most westerners as well as the climate and geography of the remaining territories had made popular sovereignty in fact a road to freedom, the moral issue was also essential to Lincoln's political campaign against Douglas. For Lincoln, expediency and principle were identical just as they had been for Douglas when confronted with the LeCompton constitution.

The famous debates which followed gave the Republican party a new national leader and a new program—ultimate extinction to begin with containment. Lincoln, however, insisted vehemently that he had no designs against slavery where it already existed and that he would not oppose the fugitive slave act. Lincoln charged throughout the debates that Douglas had been part of a deliberate conspiracy to nationalize slavery. Douglas answered by citing the active opposition of Buchanan's friends in Illinois, the free status of Kansas, and his own opposition to the LeCompton constitution. In turn the Little Giant used the "house divided" speech to show that Lincoln was promoting sectional conflict over a meaningless question since slavery could expand no further under any circumstances. Douglas shamelessly appealed to racial prejudice. Lincoln accepted the validity of racial supremacy and denied that he had

150

ever advocated or believed in political or social equality for Negroes. There was, however, a strong difference in the tone of the two racial philosophies, however similar, and Lincoln at least contradicted himself occasionally by insisting that all men regardless of race or color should have an equal right to earn a living.

In effect, Douglas argued that slavery could not and would not be extended, while Lincoln insisted that slavery should not and must not be extended. At Freeport, Illinois, Douglas answered Lincoln by restating the doctrine he had already expressed several times before. By virtue of the Dred Scott decision, he reasoned, slaveholders with slaves could not be barred from entering any territory by the federal government. This right, however, would be meaningless if local territorial legislatures refused to enact the police regulations necessary to protect the slaveholder's right to slave property. Thus, said Douglas, regardless of the Court's edict, territorial legislatures could effectively bar slavery during the territorial stage.

Southern leaders would admit no such territorial right before the actual point of application for statehood. Still, before his opposition to the LeCompton constitution, Douglas had stated his Freeport view without significant Southern criticism. Indeed, various Southerners, including Jefferson Davis, had on different occasions stated the same opinion in refuting the charge that they were trying to seize the West for slavery. The Freeport doctrine of 1858 was probably the excuse rather than the reason for the angry storm against Douglas in the South. The real crime of Douglas in Southern eyes was his cooperation with the hated Republicans against the LeCompton constitution.

Douglas won reelection to the Senate, but Lincoln had gained national stature and had given the Republican party the doctrine of ultimate extinction. With magnificent eloquence Lincoln had expressed the highest moral ideals in language which required no sacrifice from anyone. Indeed, Lincoln considered himself and his principles well-calculated to lead America toward sectional peace. If the popular conscience could be soothed by the belief that slavery could not expand, he argued, the antislavery agitation would become unnecessary and would probably cease.

The Southern support Douglas would need for the presidential election of 1860 had been further eroded, but the Little Giant had had no choice. He could not have held his even more important Northern supporters had he spoken any differently. In September, 1859, Douglas wooed the North still further with an article in *Harper's Weekly* which reiterated the Freeport doctrine in only slightly different language. The Southern press again rang with angry denunciations against the only friendly Northern leader who had a chance to keep the hated Republicans from winning the White House in 1860.

XI

The Cold War and John Brown

> The South has acted . . . according to the almost
> universal usage of civilized mankind and the in-
> junctions of the Bible. . . . She flourishes like the
> bay tree, whilst Europe starves, and she is as re-
> markable for her exemption from crime as her
> freedom from poverty. She is by far . . . the most
> prosperous and happy country in the world. Her
> jealous and dependent rivals have begun to imitate
> her. They must soon openly approve her course in
> order to vindicate themselves.
>
> GEORGE FITZHUGH

Those who loved the Union were indeed star-crossed. A brief
but painful commercial depression in 1857, which idled fifty
thousand workers in New York City alone, reflected the usual
American problem of a money and credit system inadequate
for the resources, talents, and dreams of the American people.
The industrial North suffered much; the agrarian South far less.
Earlier in the year, Southern and certain northwestern mem-

153

The Death of Slavery

bers of Congress had passed a free-trade tariff bill, and Northerners were quick to blame their troubles on this legislation. The actual need for tariff protection was less than northeasterners thought, but this further domination of the Congress by the slave power brought more Northern speeches and editorials against slavery. The South responded with the usual hurt feelings and anger. When the hapless Buchanan vetoed another homestead act and announced his opposition to all river and harbor legislation, westerners were again roused to fury against this continued thwarting by the slavocracy of their rights and manifest destiny.

In turn, various Southern papers and leaders actually exulted in the Northern plight and argued that the situation demonstrated clearly the superiority of their own economic system. The times appeared to be uniquely appropriate for the publication of George Fitzhugh's *Cannibals All: or, Slaves without Masters*. In this work of fantasy, Fitzhugh attacked the Northern wage system as cannibalistic and boldly predicted that the North would eventually switch to slavery for the benefit of the workers themselves.

The pride and comfort gained by Southerners from Fitzhugh, however, did not equal the fear and anger roused by Hinton Rowan Helper's *Impending Crisis of the South: How to Meet It*. Helper, a North Carolinian, mixed the humanitarian antislavery arguments of Washington and Jefferson with his own harsh racism, but denounced slavery and slaveholders above all for their domination and exploitation of the vast non-slaveholding white population. The South was ignorant, poor, and backward, said Helper, and would remain so until slavery was abolished and Negroes were colonized elsewhere. Helper's open call for class warfare between rich and poor was answered by

The Cold War and John Brown

intensified racist propaganda from the slaveholding leaders. If Helper's suggestions were followed, warned Albert G. Brown of Mississippi, the Negro "will insist upon being treated as an equal—that he shall go to the white man's table and the white man to his—that he shall share the white man's bed, and the white man his—that his son shall marry the white man's daughter, and the white man's daughter his son."

In another act of defiance in the face of criticism, various Southern leaders began advocating a reopening of the African slave trade. The long-standing law prescribing the death penalty for slavers had been passed with almost unanimous support of Southerners, including John C. Calhoun, and most Southerners still opposed the trade. A few, however, answered Helper's attempt to rouse antislavery feelings among the poorer whites by arguing that the reopening of the trade would drive down prices until every small farmer could own at least one slave. The arguments probably affected more Northern abolitionists than Southerners and were answered with another barrage of criticism against all things Southern.

A more concrete aspect of the slave trade question was the failure of Southern juries to convict or even indict ship captains and owners virtually taken in the act of smuggling slaves from Africa. In several spectacular cases, usually involving flagrant cruelty toward the human cargo, slavers were released and the courts were justified by Southern arguments equating these actions with Northern refusal to enforce the fugitive slave laws.

Another Southern heretic, Representative Frank Blair of Missouri, a sponsor of Helper's book, asked Congress to acquire territory in Central or South America as a place for colonizing free Negroes and liberated slaves. In an impassioned speech which he repeated often in the years 1857–60 Blair begged

The Death of Slavery

Southerners to recognize the evils of slavery and its inevitable death and take advantage of his proposal. In a burst of double-edged racism, Blair argued that Negro inferiority dictated the removal of all freed slaves to another land, but that an influx of former slaves blessed by association with Anglo-Saxon whites would actually raise the cultural and political level of the Latin American areas where they might be sent. Even those Southerners who managed to read through to the more acceptable parts of Blair's long speeches were only infuriated by his overall message.

The election of Douglas and the emergence of Lincoln were only part of the political story of 1858. Throughout the North the Republicans swept the gubernatorial, state legislative, and congressional elections almost everywhere. There were various possible reasons. Anger against the Dred Scott decision and the encroachments, however imaginary, of the slave power played a role, but the general economic suffering must have been equally important. Northerners could express their dissatisfaction with the depression and the obvious incompetence of Buchanan only by voting for either the Republicans or the Know-Nothings, and the latter clearly had no chance for real power. Southerners, however, saw the election only as further proof of Northern hostility. Southern fire-eaters were encouraged. The election of a Republican President in 1860, they hoped fervently, would be the final proof to the Southern people that only secession and independence could save their honor and safety.

The irritations and name-calling would have practical meaning, however, only if the South resorted to overt action, and until October, 1859, the evidence indicates that the lamentations of radicals like Rhett, Yancey, Ruffin, and others, were falling upon at least half-deaf ears. Southerners who did not really want to emigrate westward with slaves and Southerners who preferred a West without Negroes if they should emigrate, remained unconvinced that the Yankees, however hateful they might be, had any really serious intentions against Southern slavery. Ultimate extinction, after all, when combined with orthodox racial views and promises to obey the Constitution, leave slavery alone, and enforce the fugitive slave act, was not a very threatening doctrine.

Southerners and Northerners who wanted peace, however, had not reckoned with John Brown, late of Osawatomie, Kansas.

Even before his last invasion of Missouri and trip to Canada with the escaped slaves, John Brown, product of a family cursed by insanity and himself a failure in various shady as well as honest wealth-seeking enterprises, had decided that the Lord had still bigger plans for his talents. He would invade Virginia, capture the federal arsenal at Harper's Ferry, call upon Virginia slaves to revolt, arm those closest at hand for the holy conflict, and march southward to coordinate the spontaneous rebellions that would naturally erupt in answer to his invitation. In case the arsenal should disappoint his expectations, he had ordered from a New England blacksmith a thousand sharp metal-pointed hand pikes said to be excellent weapons in hand to hand combat.

Brown later assured a court that he had intended only to repeat the Missouri venture on a larger scale and had intended no violence. His true intentions, however, had been committed to paper as well as outlined to numerous witnesses and supporters. He did not explain the selection of an arsenal for the initial attack, and those who remembered the severed limbs of his Kansas victims needed no explanation for the pikes.

The Death of Slavery

Had the Virginia slaves flocked to Brown's banner, Brown might have set the cause of emancipation back another century. With more luck he might have caused the deaths of a great many people of both races and thereby given Northerners a new set of reasons for believing Southern arguments that the Africans must be kept in bondage.

As it was, the expedition caused only a brief moment of excitement, a handful of innocent casualties, and the capture and execution of Brown for treason, murder, and inciting slaves to rebellion. He denied all three charges. "Had I interfered," said Brown, "in behalf of the rich, the powerful, the intelligent, the so-called great . . . or any of that class . . . it would have been all right; and every man in this court would have deemed it an act worthy of reward rather than punishment."

Brown's raid was an isolated affair led by a unique fanatic, and had Southern leaders treated it as such it might have remained a failure. The old man's Northern backers were burning evidence and running for cover in all directions, and imprisonment would have denied him the martyrdom needed for a legend. The erratic and ambitious Governor Henry Wise of Virginia, however, prevented an examination for insanity, and dramatized in every possible way both the conspiracy and his own role in thwarting it. In the face of death, Brown spoke with moving eloquence and behaved with magnificent valor. His last hours gave his life and death a symbolic meaning which enabled many Northerners to forget his past crimes and cruelties. Imaginative writers, including Victor Hugo, were soon rewriting Brown's life to put it all in character with his death. Henry David Thoreau, for example, wrote:

Some eighteen hundred years ago Christ was crucified. This morning, perchance, Captain Brown was hung. These are the two ends of a chain which is not without its links. He is not Old Brown any longer; he is an angel of light. I see now that it was necessary that the bravest and humanest man in all the country should be hung. . . . I *almost fear* that I may yet hear of his deliverance, doubting if a prolonged life, if *any* life, can do as much good as his death.

As at least one observer noted, it was much easier to put him on a scaffold than to get him off.

Brown's exploit swept Southerners into a state of irrationality from which most of them never recovered. For the first time, the fire-eaters had proof that Calhoun and his successors had been right—that the North really did intend to invade the South and incite the slaves to a bloody revolt. Edmund Ruffin gathered up the pikes for exhibition to his audiences as he traveled around the South on his pilgrimage to rouse people to their danger. Politicians, newspapers, and ministers reminded Southerners of the horrible race war in Haiti half a century earlier. Brown was indeed a godsend to the Southern radicals, and in the end they completed his work. The South ultimately did to itself what the North if unprovoked by a war for disunion might never have done.

Southerners demanded a disavowal of Brown from the North, and at first all but a few ultraradicals criticized him sharply. Poets and essayists like Emerson, Thoreau, Whittier, Bryant, and others, however, saw the deed in another light, and Northern pulpits were soon dedicating hymns to the memory of St. John the Just. However insane and cruel he had been on occasion, Brown had died like a hero for a worthy cause, and his story was a magnet for literary talents seeking a dramatic theme.

Naturally enough, Southerners considered any defense of Brown a wicked attitude shared by the entire North. Southern

The Death of Slavery

voices of reason found the going hard after John Brown. The martyred murderer had struck a nerve in the minds and hearts of the great Southern majority of non-slaveholders who were ready to believe the worst about slave character and succumb to fears often more intense than those of people who actually owned and had contact with the slave population.

XII

Secession

> I have no purpose directly or indirectly to inter-
> fere with the institution of slavery in the States
> where it exists. I believe I have no lawful right to
> do so, and I have no inclination to do so.
>
> ABRAHAM LINCOLN, 1858, AND
> REPEATED IN FIRST INAUGURAL
> ADDRESS

As the fateful year 1860 began, Senator Jefferson Davis set the
tone with a set of resolutions for the consideration of his
colleagues. The federal government, he argued, was obligated
to give slavery all needful protection in the territories. The
people in the territories should have no say on the matter until
the coming of statehood, although even Davis still admitted that
at the moment of statehood any area could decide for itself.

In effect, Davis was insisting upon a federal slave code and
rejecting popular sovereignty and its author. A presidential
election lay just ahead, and since the hated Douglas had taken

a stand which should have been acceptable to any thinking Southerner, Davis and his friends had to approach the limits of absurdity to find a base for their opposition. Douglas more than held his own in the ensuing debates, but the radical Southern press again oversimplified his arguments and turned them into the words of an enemy of the South.

In the harmonious party atmosphere of 1856, the Democrats had awarded the 1860 convention to Charleston, South Carolina. The choice was fatal. Flower-bedecked Charleston in April, with the plantation families, including their beautiful daughters, in for the glittering social season, seemed to personify all that was best in the civilization glorified by the Southern ultras. Every local popular pressure played into the hands of the radicals as they methodically set about to destroy the political party they could no longer rule.

Northern Democrats came to Charleston to nominate Stephen A. Douglas and write popular sovereignty into the national platform. William L. Yancey of Alabama, Robert B. Rhett of South Carolina, Edmund Ruffin of Virginia, and their friends had other ideas. They would demand an unattainable plank calling for federal protection of slavery in all territories, and they would bolt the convention and split the party in retaliation for their failure. The inconsistency of simultaneous demands for a federal government too weak to bar slavery but strong enough to impose it upon unwilling territories bothered them not at all. They had already abandoned any real hope of further slave territories within the bounds of the United States, but to the South lay Cuba, Mexico, Central America, and other island areas which might be taken once their natural talents and energies were liberated from restricting Northern influences. They would choose their own candidate, who would be de-

Secession

feated by a black Republican, and the Southern people would then recognize the need for a final separation.

Largely because of his hatred for Douglas, President Buchanan cooperated fully. Democratic officeholders obligated to Buchanan could easily be made to understand that the elevation of Douglas to the leadership of the party would put Democratic unionists in control of the federal patronage. Whether or not, as some have believed, the nomination of Douglas before the platform debate would have changed the result, Old Buck played a major role in blocking this arrangement.

Driven to new heights of blazing oratory by the cheering galleries, Yancey and his friends recited their catalogue of alleged Northern oppressions and Southern wrongs. In the end, however, protection for territorial slavery was voted out and popular sovereignty was voted in. In a great scene of dramatic excitement, the delegations from the Deep South took their cues and marched out, and the Democratic party, America's last great bond of national unity, was torn apart. Within a few weeks, the Northern Democrats had nominated Douglas, while the bolters had turned to Vice-President John Breckinridge of Kentucky.

Somewhat later, a group of former Southern Whigs still unwilling to cooperate with Democrats joined forces with former Northern Whigs averse both to Republican radicalism and to former Democrats turned Free-Soil Republicans. The result was the Constitutional Union party, liberally spiced also with Know Nothings, which nominated John Bell of Tennessee.

The Republicans, meanwhile, had convened in Chicago with their great New York leader, William Henry Seward, as the obvious choice. In February, 1860, Seward countered his

163

earlier "higher law" and "irrepressible conflict" doctrines with a widely publicized plea for tolerance and sectional harmony. While Seward sincerely disliked slavery, his role of radical abolitionist had never been much more than a pose assumed for the practical purpose of winning elections.

Seward's discovery that the sectional differences were essentially economic rather than moral came too late, however. In the same month, the ungainly but eloquent prairie lawyer Abraham Lincoln delivered a masterly address at Cooper's Union in New York City. With a brilliantly delivered argument documenting the right and the duty of the federal government to restrict territorial slavery, Lincoln stirred the moral sensibilities of his cheering audience. With a sharp repudiation of John Brown and a long list of assurances to the South that the territorial restriction in no way threatened slavery in its present habitat, he demonstrated his good sense and safeness to a Northern audience spreading far beyond his immediate listeners. "Wrong as we think slavery is," said Lincoln, "we can yet afford to let it alone where it is, because that much is due to the necessity arising from its actual presence in the nation." Still, Lincoln concluded, the North must never compromise to the point of admitting the rightness of slavery. The speech was a sensation, and while his words were still echoing in the press, Lincoln repeated them in several more addresses in New England.

When the Republican convention met in May, a throng of Sewardites from New York paraded through the streets of Chicago behind their own brass band—while noisy Lincoln supporters shrewdly grabbed off the gallery seats in the Wigwam. Seward's enemies combined against him, while the more conservative Lincoln, with his strong western support, had

Suggested Reading

Southern Negroes, 1861–1865 (1938), *The Plain People of the South* (1943); H. H. Cunningham, *Doctors in Gray* (1958); George W. Adams, *Doctors in Blue: The Medical History of the Union Army* (1952); Margaret Leech, *Reveille in Washington* (1941); and Bernard Weisberger, *Reporters for the Union* (1943).

The relations of the belligerents with Europe are described by E. D. Adams, *Great Britain and the American Civil War* (2 vols., 1925 and 1957); Donaldson Jordan and E. J. Pratt, *Europe and the American Civil War* (1931); Frank L. Owsley, *King Cotton Diplomacy* (1931 and 1959); Frederic Bancroft, *The Life of William H. Seward* (2 vols., 1900); Margaret Clapp, *Forgotten First Citizen: John Bigelow* (1947); and M. B. Duberman, *Charles Francis Adams, 1807–1889* (1961).

The biographies of this period offer many fascinating details and perceptive interpretations. The enormous Lincoln bibliography is graced by such works as Benjamin P. Thomas, *Abraham Lincoln* (1952); Reinhard H. Luthin, *The Real Abraham Lincoln* (1960); James G. Randall, *Lincoln the President* (4 vols., 1945–55), with Richard N. Current as co-author of Volume IV; Current, *Mr. Lincoln* (1957) and *The Lincoln Nobody Knows* (1958); Carl Sandburg, *Abraham Lincoln: The War Years* (4 vols., 1949), and *Abraham Lincoln* (1954); David Donald, *Lincoln Reconsidered: Essays on the Civil War Era* (1956); Albert Beveridge, *Abraham Lincoln 1809–1858* (2 vols., 1928); and J. G. Nicolay and John Hay, *Abraham Lincoln: A History* (10 vols., 1890; abridged ed. 1966). Nicolay and Hay were Lincoln's secretaries and offer many firsthand accounts of controversial events. Roy P. Basler, *The Collected Works of Abraham Lincoln* (9 vols., 1953), is a basic original source. Specialized Lincoln studies and monographs include Burton J. Hendrick, *Lincoln's War Cabinet* (1946); William B. Hesseltine, *Lincoln and the War Governors* (1948); Harry J. Carman and Reinhard J. Luthin, *Lincoln and the Patronage* (1943); T. Harry Williams, *Lincoln and the Radicals* (1941); R. S. Harper, *Lincoln and the Press* (1951); R. V. Bruce, *Lincoln and the Tools of War* (1956); C. R. Ballard, *The Military Genius of Abraham Lincoln* (1952); a brilliant reappraisal by Don E. Fehrenbacher, *Prelude to Greatness: Lincoln in the 1850's* (1962); and William E. Barringer, *Lincoln's Rise to Power* (1937), and *A House Dividing* (1945).

Calhoun receives friendly and favorable treatment from Charles

213

The Death of Slavery

M. Wiltse, *John C. Calhoun, Nullifier, 1829–1839* (1949), and *John C. Calhoun, Sectionalist, 1840–1850* (1951); and Margaret L. Coit, *John C. Calhoun: American Portrait* (1950). More critical and more realistic are Richard N. Current, *John C. Calhoun* (1963); G. M. Capers, *John C. Calhoun—Opportunist: A Reappraisal* (1960); and Richard Hofstadter in the Calhoun chapter of *The American Political Tradition and the Men Who Made It* (1948).

Thomas Hart Benton, the bitter enemy of Calhoun, has been recently portrayed by E. B. Smith, *Magnificent Missourian: The Life of Thomas Hart Benton* (1958), and William N. Chambers, *Old Bullion Benton, Senator from the New West: Thomas Hart Benton* (1956).

Henry Clay, the great peacemaker, is perhaps best described by Carl Schurz, *Henry Clay* (2 vols., 1899); Glyndon G. Van Deusen, *Life of Henry Clay* (1937); and Clement Eaton, *Henry Clay and the Art of American Politics* (1957). The latter work captures the real essence of Clay's contribution.

Daniel Webster receives his due from Charles M. Fuess, *Daniel Webster* (2 vols., 1930), and Richard N. Current, *Daniel Webster and the Rise of National Conservatism* (1955). A highly readable popular study which leans heavily upon biographical analysis is Gerald W. Johnson, *America's Silver Age: The Statecraft of Clay, Webster, and Calhoun* (1939).

The latest study of Douglas is G. M. Capers, *Stephen A. Douglas, Defender of the Union* (1959), and others are in progress. The older book by Allen Johnson, *Stephen A. Douglas* (1908), and the previously cited George F. Milton, *The Eve of Conflict: Stephen A. Douglas and the Needless War* (1934), are adequate. See also *Created Equal? The Complete Lincoln-Douglas Debates of 1858* (1958), edited by Paul M. Angle; and H. V. Jaffa, *Crisis of the House Divided: An Interpretation of the Issues in the Lincoln-Douglas Debates* (1959).

Other valuable studies of Northern leaders include David Donald, *Charles Sumner and the Coming of the Civil War* (1960); Ralph V. Harlow, *Gerrit Smith, Philanthropist and Reformer* (1939); R. L. Rusk, *The Life of Ralph Waldo Emerson* (1949); Allan Nevins, *Frémont, Pathmarker of the West* (1955); F. B. Woodford, *Lewis Cass* (1950); Robert J. Rayback, *Millard Fillmore* (1959); Glyndon G. Van Deusen, *Thurlow Weed* (1947) and *Horace Greeley* (1953);

Suggested Reading

W. H. Hale, *Horace Greeley, Voice of the People* (1950); Frederic Bancroft, *William H. Seward* (2 vols., 1900); Roy F. Nichols, *Franklin Pierce, Young Hickory of the Granite Plains* (1931); O. G. Villard, *John Brown, 1800–1859: A Biography Fifty Years After* (1910); R. P. Warren, *John Brown: The Making of a Martyr* (1929); James C. Malin, *John Brown and the Legend of Fifty-six* (1942); P. S. Klein, *President James Buchanan* (1962); Hans L. Trefousse, *Benjamin Franklin Wade* (1963); Richard N. Current, *Old Thad Stevens* (1942); Benjamin P. Thomas and H. M. Hyman, *Stanton* (1962); Thomas G. and Marva R. Belden, *So Fell the Angels* (1956), a study of Salmon P. Chase; Don E. Fehrenbacher, *Chicago Giant, a Biography of "Long John" Wentworth* (1957); and Holman Hamilton, *Zachary Taylor, Soldier in the White House* (1951). While he was originally a Southerner, Taylor must be considered a pro-Northern President.

Colorful but scholarly biographies of Southern leaders include Burton J. Hendrick, *Statesmen of the Lost Cause* (1939); Gamaliel Bradford, *Confederate Portraits* (1914); William E. Dodd, *Jefferson Davis* (1907); Hudson Strode, *Jefferson Davis: American Patriot* (1955); H. J. Eckenrode, *Jefferson Davis, President of the South* (1923); Avery O. Craven, *Edmund Ruffin, Southerner* (1932); Broadus Mitchell, *William Gregg* (1928); Laura A. White, *Robert Barnwell Rhett: Father of Secession* (1931); Ulrich B. Phillips, *Robert Toombs* (1913); O. C. Skipper, *J. D. B. DeBow: Magazinist of the Old South* (1958); D. L. Smiley, *Lion of White Hall: The Life of Cassius M. Clay* (1962); Louis Pendleton, *Alexander H. Stephens* (1908); Rudolph von Abele, *Alexander H. Stephens* (1946); R. D. Meade, *Judah P. Benjamin* (1943); W. E. Parrish, *David Rice Atchison* (1961); and Oliver B. Chitwood, *John Tyler* (1939).

James K. Polk has been perceptively studied by Charles G. Sellers, *James K. Polk, Jacksonian* (1957), and Ernest I. McCormac, *James K. Polk* (1922). The final Polk volume by Sellers is eagerly awaited. Marquis James, *The Raven* (1929), is an exciting account of Sam Houston. Joseph H. Parks, *John Bell of Tennessee* (1950), describes still another Southern moderate. (See also the two published editions of Polk's diary of his presidential years by Milo M. Quaife [4 vols., 1910] and Allan Nevins [1929]).

Among the better military biographies are C. W. Elliot, *Winfield Scott* (1937); Holman Hamilton, *Zachary Taylor, Soldier of the*

The Death of Slavery

Republic (1946); Douglas S. Freeman, *R. E. Lee* (4 vols., 1934–35); Burke Davis, *Gray Fox* (1956); Frank Vandiver, *Mighty Stonewall* (1957); T. Harry Williams, *Beauregard, Napoleon in Gray* (1955); R. S. Henry, *"First with the Most" Forrest* (1944); J. W. Thomason, Jr., *Jeb Stuart* (1930); J. P. Dyer, *The Gallant Hood* (1950); J. F. C. Fuller, *The Generalship of Ulysses S. Grant* (1929); Bruce Catton, *Grant Moves South* (1960); Freeman Cleaves, *The Rock of Chickamauga* (1948)—a study of G. H. Thomas; W. S. Myers, *A Study in Personality, General George Brinton McClellan* (1934); H. J. Eckenrode and Bryan Conrad, *George B. McClellan* (1941); W. W. Hassler, Jr., *General George B. McClellan* (1957); Lloyd Lewis, *Sherman, Fighting Prophet* (1932); Richard O'Connor, *Sheridan the Inevitable* (1953); T. Harry Williams, *McClellan, Sherman and Grant* (1962); W. A. Roberts, *Semmes of the Alabama* (1938); and C. L. Lewis, *David Glasgow Farragut* (2 vols., 1941–43). A biography of Admiral Samuel Phillips Lee is needed.

To all of the many authors whose able and valuable works are omitted from the foregoing list I humbly apologize.

Acknowledgments

I am grateful to many who have helped me write this book.
To the librarians and curators who make the writing of history possible.

To Avery Craven, William T. Hutchinson, Walter Johnson, Verton Queener, Jessie Heron, and Effie C. Huffaker, for their teaching.

To the many authors from whom I have gained information and insight.

To the Social Science Research Council for financial assistance on a related subject which added to my knowledge of this one.

To Michael Collins who suggested the radio lectures which became the first draft of this book, and to station WOI, Ames, Iowa, for broadcasting them.

To Colonel E. Brooke Lee for hospitality and information.

To Betty Jean McCormick and Susan Palmer for typing, to Kathleen Hall for proofreading, and to Carole Kennedy for cheerful assistance.

To Clarence H. Matterson for kindness and patience.

To my fellow politicians who make those of the nineteenth century easier to understand.

To my wife, Jean, for unselfishness, assistance, encouragement, and inspiration.

Index

Blair, Francis P., 44, 45, 54, 55, 57, 60, 70, 72, 73, 80, 81, 98, 136, 138, 172–73
Blair, Frank, 155–56, 165, 166
Blair, James, 45
Blair, Montgomery, 173
"Bleeding Kansas," 131 ff.
"Bleeding Sumner," 135 ff.
Bragg, Braxton (General), 183
Breckinridge, John, 163, 165–66, 167
Brook Farm, 16
Brooks, Preston, 135, 137
Brown, Albert G., 155
Brown, John, 37, 39, 117–18, 133, 157–60, 164, 166
Bryant, William Cullen, 55, 98, 137, 138, 159
Buchanan, James, 18, 32, 61, 82, 83, 91, 92, 124, 126, 139, 141–48, 150, 154, 156, 163, 169
Bull Run, Battle of, 177, 178, 187
Burns, Anthony, 117
Burnside, Ambrose (General), 179, 188
Butler, Andrew Pickens III, 134–35
Butler, Benjamin F., 79, 89–90, 124, 188

Calhoun, John C., 6, 7, 25, 33, 41, 46 ff., 53, 56, 61, 63, 66–73, 81, 83, 84, 86, 92–99, 104–10, 155, 159
California, 32, 76, 81, 82, 87, 88, 90, 91, 95, 99–100, 103, 104, 106, 108, 109, 111, 113, 126, 138
Calvinism, 12, 13, 15
Cambreling, C. C., 98
Cameron, Simon, 111, 138, 165, 166
Cannibals All: or, Slaves without Masters, 154
Cass, Lewis, 61, 96, 98, 124, 128
Chancellorsville, Battle of, 179
Chandler, Zachariah, 138, 186
Channing, William Ellery, 15
Charleston, South Carolina, 162, 172–74
Chase, Salmon P., 98, 109, 128, 138
Chicago Tribune, 44, 123, 134

Chickamauga, Battle of, 183
Christian Perfectionism, 40
Cilley-Graves duel, 45
Clark, William P., 118
Clay, Henry, 31, 45, 48–53, 56, 58–60, 69, 73, 85, 97–99, 103–4, 107–14, 124–25, 195, 196
Cobb, Howell, 103
Coffin, Levi, 35
Coles, Edward, 35
Compromise of 1850, 7, 98 ff., 125, 128
Confederate States of America, 169, 170, 172, 177, 182, 193
Conquest of Kansas, by Missouri and Her Allies, 133
Conscience Whigs, 98
Constitutional Union Party, 163
Contract Labor Law, 197
Cooke, Jay, 196
Cooper Union speech, 164
Cornish, Dudley T., *The Sable Arm*, 192
Corwin, Thomas, 85
Craft, William and Ellen, 116–17
Craven, Avery, 10, 54, 168
Crittenden, John J., 170
Crothers, Samuel, 35
Cuba, 86, 126
Curtis, B. R., 145
Curtis, George W., 165
Cushing, Caleb, 125

Dahlgren, John (Commodore), 180
Daily Union, 103
Dana, R. H., 37
Dartmouth College, 37
Davis, Jefferson, 6, 97, 99, 108–9, 111, 114, 125, 127, 128, 151, 161, 177, 183
Declaration of Independence, 6, 36, 38, 165
Democratic Party, 19, 26, 31, 32, 56, 58–59, 60, 61, 70, 72, 74, 79, 80, 92, 96, 97–98, 123–24, 126, 139, 162–63, 167
District of Columbia, 41, 50, 55, 101, 103, 190

Index

Dixon, Archibald, 128
Dodd, William E., 8
Donelson, Andrew J., 80
Douglas, Stephen A., 28, 32, 114, 124, 125, 126 ff., 135, 139, 146, 147–52, 156, 161–63, 165–67, 169, 170
Dred Scott case, 7, 144–47, 151, 156, 167
DuPont, Samuel T. (Commodore), 180

Eaton, John and Peggy, 47
Elections, presidential, 1840, 58 ff.; 1844, 69 ff.; 1848, 97 ff.; 1852, 123 ff.; 1856, 138 ff.; 1860, 162 ff.
Elliott, Charles (Captain), 64
Emancipation Proclamation, 176–77, 190–91
Emerson, Ralph Waldo, 16, 37, 137, 159
Evarts, William M., 137
Everett, Edward, 64, 66, 137

Farragut, David (Admiral), 182
Fifteenth Amendment, 6
Fillmore, Millard, 112, 113, 140
Finney, Charles G., 40
Fitzhugh, George, 153, 154
Florida, C.S.S., 180–81
Foote, Henry S., 95, 101, 111–12, 113, 114
Fort Donelson, 183
Fort Henry, 183
Fort Pickens, 172, 174
Fort Sumter, 1, 172–74, 180, 184
Fourteenth Amendment, 6
Fox, Gustavus, 173
France, 110, 126, 173
Fredericksburg, Battle of, 179
Freeport doctrine, 151–52
Free-Soil Party, 17, 92, 93, 98, 138, 168
Free-Soilers, 40, 103, 147, 163
Frémont, John C., 4, 87–88, 90, 100, 138–42, 188, 190
Frémont, Mrs. John C., 87, 141
Fruitlands, 16

Fugitive slave laws, 4, 102, 103, 104, 107, 111, 115, 116 ff., 125, 155, 157, 165, 167, 170

Gadsden Purchase, 125–26
Gardner, David, 67
Garner, Margaret, 117
Garrison, William Lloyd, 6, 27, 34, 37, 38, 39, 130
Gettysburg Address, 5, 52, 185
Gettysburg, Battle of, 5, 179, 183, 185, 188
Giddings, Joshua, 84, 116, 165
Gilmer, Thomas, 67
Globe, The Washington, 44, 54, 56, 67, 69, 73, 78, 80
Goliad massacre, 62
Gorsuch (Maryland slaveholder killed in Pennsylvania), 117
Grant, Ulysses S., 135, 180, 182–84, 188, 193
Great Britain, 29, 46, 64–65, 68, 81, 82, 83, 110, 116, 126, 139, 173, 179, 181–82, 190
Greeley, Horace, 4, 27, 138, 148, 149, 166, 190
Green, Duff, 45, 47, 48, 64
Greenbacks, 196–97
Grimké sisters, 35, 37
Grinnell, Josiah Bushnell, 118

Haiti, 21, 159
Hale, John, 94–95, 109
Halleck, Henry (General), 178
Hamilton, Alexander, 8, 195–97
Hammond, James, 69
Harper's Ferry, 157
Harper's Weekly, 152
Harrison, William Henry, 31, 57, 60
Hartford Convention of 1815, 52
Helper, Hinton Rowan, 154–55
H. L. Hunley, C.S.S., 181
Holmes, Oliver Wendell, 137
Homesteads, 98, 154, 165, 197
Hooker, Joseph (General), 179, 188
Hopkins, John H. (Bishop), 37
Housatonic, U.S.S., 181

221

Index

Index

THE CHICAGO HISTORY OF AMERICAN CIVILIZATION

DANIEL J. BOORSTIN, EDITOR

Edmund S. Morgan, *The Birth of the Republic: 1763–89*

Marcus Cunliffe, *The Nation Takes Shape: 1789–1837*

John Hope Franklin, *Reconstruction: After the Civil War*

Samuel P. Hays, *The Response to Industrialism: 1885–1914*

William E. Leuchtenburg, *The Perils of Prosperity: 1914–32*

Dexter Perkins, *The New Age of Franklin Roosevelt: 1932–45*

Herbert Agar, *The Price of Power: America since 1945*

* * *

Robert H. Bremner, *American Philanthropy*

Harry L. Coles, *The War of 1812*

Richard M. Dorson, *American Folklore*

John Tracy Ellis, *American Catholicism*

Nathan Glazer, *American Judaism*

William T. Hagan, *American Indians*

Winthrop S. Hudson, *American Protestantism*

Maldwyn Allen Jones, *American Immigration*

Robert G. McCloskey, *The American Supreme Court*

Howard H. Peckham, *The War for Independence: A Military History*

Howard H. Peckham, *The Colonial Wars: 1689–1762*

Henry Pelling, *American Labor*

*John B. Rae, *The American Automobile: A Brief History*

Charles P. Roland, *The Confederacy*

Otis A. Singletary, *The Mexican War*

John F. Stover, *American Railroads*

*Bernard A. Weisberger, *The American Newspaperman*

* Available in cloth only. All other books published in both cloth and paperback editions.